Young Person's Guide to Getting & Keeping a Good Job

Second Edition

J. Michael Farr

Marie A. Pavlicko, Ed.D.

Gayle O. MacDonald, M.Ed.

Young Person's Guide to Getting & Keeping a Good Job, Second Edition

© 2000 by JIST Publishing, Inc.

Except for the material in Chapter 8 that appears in *Creating Your High School Resume: A Step-by-Step Guide to Preparing an Effective Resume for College and Career* (JIST Works). © 1998 by Kathryn Kraemer Troutman. All rights reserved. Used with permission.

Published by JIST Works, an imprint of JIST Publishing, Inc.
8902 Otis Avenue
Indianapolis, IN 46216-1033

Phone: 1-800-648-JIST   Fax: 1-800-JIST-FAX

E-mail: info@jist.com   Web site: www.jist.com

Important Note to Instructors

This workbook was written to support a course on career planning, job search methods, and job survival skills for high school juniors and seniors. The course can be presented as a minicurriculum within other courses or as a separate course.

An instructor's guide (ISBN 1-56370-633-4) is available separately to support this workbook and is essential for its presentation in class or group settings. It will save you many hours of session planning. This comprehensive guide contains activities to support each chapter, including discussion topics, assignments, and more.

A separate book of transparencies (ISBN 1-56370-594-X) reinforces all major topics covered in the student workbook. The transparencies are excellent for seminars, workshops, and large classes.

Also available separately is the *Data Minder* (ISBN 1-56370-595-8), which is attached to the inside back cover of this book.

Quantity discounts are available for JIST books. Call 1-800-648-5478 for a free catalog and more information.

Development Editor: Susan Pines
Cover and Interior Designer: Aleata Howard
Proofreader: Rebecca York

Printed in the United States of America

04 03 02 01   9 8 7 6 5 4 3

ISBN 1-56370-555-9

About This Book

This workbook will show you how to find a good job—even if you don't have paid work experience yet. What is a good job? Most people would agree that one element of a good job is that it suits your skills and interests. You will learn how to identify your skills and take the other steps important in your job search.

While this book assumes you have some idea about what you want to do, the material will be helpful even if you don't know or are looking for part-time or summer work. In addition, the appendix shows you how to get started in career exploration.

Through clear explanations, worksheets, and examples, this book will help you do the following:

- Understand an employer's expectations.
- Discover and present your skills.
- Document your work and school experiences.
- Learn effective job search techniques.
- Do a good job on applications, cover letters, and your resume.

- Find references who can talk about your skills.
- Handle yourself well in interviews.
- Answer even the toughest interview questions.
- Create a portfolio.
- Organize your schedule to get a good job in less time.
- Get ahead on a new job.

The small *Data Minder* attached to the inside back cover of this workbook lets you record the details needed during your job search. Fill it in, carry it with you, and use it as you complete applications, do your resume, and go on interviews.

We hope this workbook helps you learn some good things about yourself—and helps you get off to a good start in your career and your life. We wish you well.

Contents

Preface

You are fortunate to attend a program that teaches you the material in this workbook. Most people are not so fortunate. None of the authors, for example, was taught anything about job seeking in high school or college. None took a career test. In short, no one helped us with our career or job search planning. We turned out well, but it would have been much easier if we had been offered this type of training.

While this book is easy to use, you should know that the content is based on extensive research on the most effective job search methods and job survival skills available. Millions of people have used the JIST job search techniques to find better jobs in less time. The techniques we recommend *do* work. But they will work only if you are willing to use them. If you plan to get a full-time, part-time, or summer job in the next few months or years, this workbook will help. We wrote it to give you the basics you need to obtain a new job and to do it well.

Even if you don't plan to look for a job soon, the material is important for other reasons. It will encourage you to think about what you want out of life and what you have to offer. Can you, for example, list your skills? Can you tell someone what you do well? You will learn to answer these questions—and many more.

The first edition of this book was tested with thousands of students before it was published, and many more thousands have used it since. Those students, as well as their teachers, have helped us improve this edition. Thanks for your enthusiasm! The editors and designers at JIST have also helped greatly in making the book look and "work" better.

The second edition contains many new and improved features, including the following:

- Information on using the Internet and technology in your job search.

- More details on interviewing, including preparation, appearance, and behavior.

- Many answers to difficult interview questions.

- More resume and JIST Card examples for young people.

- Examples of well-completed job applications.

- More information on choosing and listing references.

- New chapter with step-by-step information on writing cover letters.

- New chapter on portfolios, featuring examples of what to include.

- Details on how to decide on a job offer.

- New design; roomier worksheets; revised and reorganized for easy reading and use.

- Page references where appropriate to the *Data Minder* booklet for easy information transfer.

Let's get started!

CHAPTER 1

An Introduction to Finding a Good Job

You probably already know some things about finding a job. Perhaps you have found part-time jobs in the past. Your job now is to learn how to find a good job and how to find it in less time.

Before looking for a job, you must know how to identify the skills you have and learn some new ones. You should have some idea of what type of job you are qualified for. Finally, you must learn how to improve the job search techniques you already know.

Job-Seeking Skills Can Improve Your Career and Your Life

During the years you work, you will probably change jobs and even careers many times. Knowing how to find a good job is a valuable skill that can make a difference in your career and your life.

Many job seekers have never learned effective job-seeking skills. In fact, most have never read a book on how to find a job. As a result, they often are unemployed far longer than they need to be. And they often take jobs that don't give them the pay and satisfaction another job might.

Job-seeking skills can help you obtain more rewarding jobs throughout your life.

Activity

The Job Search Quiz

This quiz is designed to help you discover what you know about looking for work. It will also help you think about your job search. Your answers will not be graded. Read each question carefully and answer it as well as you can.

1. Name five reasons why people stay unemployed.

   _____

   _____

   _____

   _____

   _____

2. What are the top three reasons that employers give for screening out (not hiring) job seekers? _____

   _____

   _____

   _____

3. List five of your best or most important skills. (Note: These skills don't have to be job related. They should be things you do particularly well.) _____

   _____

   _____

   _____

_____

_____

_____

4. What are the two most effective techniques for finding a job? _____

_____

_____

_____

5. How many hours per week should you invest in a job search? _____

6. What percentage of all jobs is advertised? _____

7. What is the real purpose of an application form? _____

_____

_____

_____

8. What size organizations hire the most people? _____

9. How many weeks is the average job seeker unemployed? _____

10. Guess how often the average person changes jobs: _____

11. How often will the average worker change careers in his or her lifetime?

_____

12. What is the employment rate in your region? _____

You will learn the answers to these and other questions in this course. Some answers may surprise you. You will learn that the more you know about yourself and the job market, the more likely you will find a good job.

Getting a Job *Is* a Job

Getting a job is a job in itself. The harder you work at it, the better your chances are of getting the job you want.

Like other things you have learned, this course will require some effort. But the advantages to you are great. Whether you are presently working, looking for work, planning to enter the job market after graduation, or planning to further your education beyond high school, you need to know the basics of how to find a job.

This course will show you how to organize your job search to get better results. Thousands of people have used these job search methods to find better jobs in less time. So can you.

CHAPTER 2

An Employer's Expectations

Sometimes, the best way to know what employers expect of you is to find out what they look for in other job seekers. This chapter will teach you to think like an employer and examine just what employers look for in the people they hire.

The important question you need to answer is "Do I meet an employer's expectations?"

Activity

What Does an Employer Expect?

In this activity, you will work with a small group of other students to form your own company. You are to complete the following tasks:

1. Appoint a group member to be a company recorder. The recorder will write down all the ideas your group comes up with on the following worksheet.

2. Give your group a company name and product or service.

3. Make a list of the positions your company needs to fill.

4. Make a list of points you think are important to look for in potential employees. Make your list as long as possible. Try to list 15 to 20 things. Your list can also include points that would prevent applicants from being hired by your company.

Employee Characteristics Worksheet

Company name: _____

Product or service: _____

_____

Types of positions your company is looking to fill: _____

_____

_____

_____

_____

List the most important points to look for in
potential employees. Don't worry if the ideas seem
good or bad. Just list every idea that your group has.

_____   _____

_____   _____

_____   _____

_____   _____

_____   _____

_____   _____

_____   _____

List key ideas from other groups:

_____   _____

_____   _____

_____   _____

_____   _____

_____   _____

Activity

The Three Major Employer Expectations

Employers know what they expect from people who apply for jobs. The important question you need to answer is "Do I meet an employer's expectations?"

Before you answer this, take a closer look at yourself and review the major points an employer looks for in an interview. The following worksheets on each expectation will help you prepare for job interviews and list the ways that you can improve.

Employer's Expectation 1— Personal Appearance

Do you look like the right person for the job?

1. How would you dress for an interview? _____

_____

_____

2. Who in the room looks like the best person for a job, based on the way he or she appears right now (sits, stands, talks, and so on)? _____

3. What special qualities about that person stand out and make him or her look like the best fit for a job? _____

_____

_____

4. What would you do to make a good first impression? _____

_____

_____

Would your manner make the interviewer want to hire you?

1. How does the way you normally act compare with the way you would act during an interview?

   _____

   _____

2. What can you do to avoid becoming nervous in an interview? _____

   _____

   _____

3. Is it better to be quiet and shy in an interview or more assertive—and possibly be seen as pushy? Why? _____

   _____

   _____

4. What interview behaviors might an employer react to in a negative way?

   _____

   _____

How else can you make an impression? How could each of the following impress an employer?

1. Your paper tools (application, resume, portfolio, and so on): _____

   _____

   _____

2. Phone conversations with the employer: _____

   _____

   _____

(continues)

(continued)

3. What others say about you: _____

_____

_____

_____

_____

 TIP

First impressions count! Did you know that of all job seekers, 40 percent get rejected because of poor personal appearance? If you do not make a positive first impression with an employer, you probably won't get hired.

Meeting Expectation 1

Write three things that you could improve to meet employer's expectation 1:

1. _____

_____

2. _____

_____

3. _____

_____

Employer's Expectation 2—Attendance, Punctuality, and Dependability

Can you be counted on to do the job?

1. Why would an employer be interested in your attendance record? _____

    _____

    _____

2. When is the best time to arrive for an interview? Why? _____

    _____

    _____

3. What does the expression "Time is money" mean to you? _____

    _____

    _____

4. Have you been reliable in the past, either in school or on a previous job?
    Give examples: _____

    _____

    _____

5. Why is an employer interested in how long you might stay on the job?

    _____

    _____

Employers will not hire you unless they are sure you are dependable and can get the job done. Someone who is unreliable or who will leave too soon after learning the job is not worth the trouble of hiring and training. Many employers will hire a person with fewer credentials over a more experienced person if they feel that the inexperienced person is more reliable.

Meeting Expectation 2

Give examples of how you would show an employer that you

1. Have a good attendance record: _____

   _____

2. Are punctual: _____

   _____

3. Are reliable: _____

   _____

Employer's Expectation 3— Skills, Experience, and Training

If you make a good first impression and convince the employer that you can be counted on (employer expectations 1 and 2), then your ability to do the job becomes important. Here are some points to consider:

1. What can you do now that relates to a job you want? _____

   _____

   _____

2. Why is the following statement not a good answer to the previous question? "I worked as a cashier at Ford two years, and I worked as a grill cook at Wendy's two years."

_____

_____

3. Will employers accept training, hobbies, and other unpaid experiences to make up for a lack of paid work experience?_____

    Why? _____

_____

4. How could you use job-related training in place of work experience to convince employers to hire you? _____

_____

_____

5. What should you do if your hobbies do not have any relationship to the job you want? What if they do? _____

_____

_____

6. What would volunteer work tell an employer about you? _____

_____

_____

7. Why is it important to translate life experiences into informal training and state them in years (or months)? _____

_____

_____

TIP

Job-related skills are important to an employer. Most employers will consider your training and other life experience to make up for shortcomings in work experience. Many employers will hire someone who they are convinced will be reliable and hard working. Employers can often train this kind of person on the job to make up for a lack of experience.

Meeting Expectation 3

Write three things you could say to an employer in an interview to help meet employer's expectation 3:

1. _____

   _____

2. _____

   _____

3. _____

   _____

Activity

Survey of Employers

This activity will give you an opportunity to learn what local employers look for. You are to visit or call at least one employer before the next class. The employer can be someone you already know—like an uncle, for example. You can also look up an employer in the yellow pages of the phone book or simply drop in on an employer on your way home from school.

As you make your call or visit, use the following survey form to record your information. You will report your findings at the next class session.

Here are some tips and important reminders:

1. Get to the person in charge.

2. List the name of the person in charge, job title, and contact information.

3. Ask the three survey questions.

4. Record the employer's responses on the survey sheet.

5. Be ready to report your findings to the class at the next session.

Employers are people, so they will react in different ways to your asking them questions. But most students who do this activity find that

- Most employers are friendly. They are willing to answer your questions.

- While employers may use different words to explain what they want in employees, it usually fits into one of the three employer expectations.

- The employers "dropped in on" might be willing to hire you and your classmates in the future!

Employer's Expectations Telephone/On-Site Survey Worksheet

Organization name: _____

Address: _____

Phone number: _____

Employer's name: _____

Employer's job title: _____

What you should do

Introduce yourself. *Hello, my name is* _____

I am a student at _____

Ask to talk to the person in charge, and find out his or her name. *May I please talk to the person in charge, or may I speak with Mr. (or Mrs. or Ms.)* _____?

When you speak to that person, introduce yourself again. Explain that you are doing an assignment for school and would like to ask a few questions about what he or she looks for in a good worker.

Ask the following three questions, and record the answers in the spaces given.

   1. Could you please tell me what you look for in a person you hire? _____

   _____

   _____

   _____

   _____

   _____

2. *What are the top three skills needed by the people who work here?*

_____

_____

_____

3. *What are the most important personality traits for people who do this type of work?* _____

_____

_____

_____

Thank the employer for the time he or she spent with you.

CHAPTER 3

Identify Your Skills

You probably don't realize how many skills you have. In fact, you probably have more than you think.

Employers want to know what skills you will bring to the job. You must be able to identify and give examples of your skills in an interview. Of all job seekers, 80 to 85 percent cannot describe their job skills in an interview. Knowing what you can do well is an important part of your job search and your life.

Three Types of Skills

How many skills do you think you have? Write your answer here:

Each person has hundreds of skills! To better understand them, let's divide them into these three categories:

- Self-management skills
- Transferable skills
- Job-related skills

Following are brief definitions of each type of skill. The activities that follow will help you identify your self-management, transferable, and job-related skills.

In these sections, be as honest and accurate about yourself as possible. Make sure that you can back up each of your skills with an example!

Self-Management Skills

Self-management skills help you adapt and do well in new situations. They include your personality, your ability to get along with others, and your ability to fit into the work situation. Some examples of using these skills include being reliable, cooperating with others, and being willing to work hard.

Transferable Skills

Transferable skills are those you can use in many different jobs. An auto mechanic, for example, needs to be good with his or her hands, and an administrative assistant must be well organized. These skills can also be used in or transferred to many other types of jobs. For example, a carpenter must be good with his or her hands, and a librarian must be well organized.

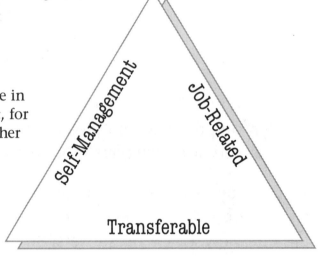

3 Types of Skills

You probably have more skills than you realize.

Job-Related Skills

Job-related skills are needed in a particular job. An auto mechanic, for example, must be familiar with tools and repair procedures, and an accountant must be know balance sheets and computerized accounting systems.

Skills Categories Not Perfect But Still Useful

The system of dividing skills into three categories is not perfect. And some things, such as being trustworthy, dependable, and well organized, are considered both personality traits and skills.

Some overlap exists between the three skills categories. For example, a skill such as being organized can be considered either a self-management or transferable skill. For our purposes, however, the skills categories are a very useful system for identifying skills that are important in the job search.

Make sure you can back up each skill with an example!

Activity

Identify Your Self-Management Skills

This activity will help you identify your self-management skills. Remember to be honest with yourself.

Good-Worker Traits

List three things about yourself that, in your opinion, make you a good worker:

1. _____

2. _____

3. _____

Self-Management Skills Checklist

Check all the skills that apply to you. Be sure you can prove your skills with specific examples.

Key Skills

All employers highly value the following skills. They often won't hire a person who does not have most or all of these skills.

_____ Dependable		_____ Hard working	
_____ Enthusiastic		_____ Honest	
_____ Follow instructions		_____ Mature	
_____ Get along well with others		_____ On time	
_____ Good attendance		_____ Responsible	
_____ Good attitude			

Other Self-Management Skills

_____ Adaptive

_____ Adventurous

_____ Ambitious

_____ Assertive

_____ Careful

_____ Cooperative

_____ Creative

_____ Dedicated

_____ Efficient

_____ Energetic

_____ Flexible

_____ Friendly

_____ Helpful

_____ Highly motivated

_____ Independent

_____ Industrious

_____ Inquisitive

_____ Intelligent

_____ Patient

_____ Persistent

_____ Physically strong

_____ Polite

_____ Quick learner

_____ Self-motivated

_____ Sense of humor

_____ Sincere

_____ Tactful

_____ Trustworthy

Additional Self-Management Skills

Add any self-management skills you have that are not in the list.

_____ _____

_____ _____

_____ _____

_____ _____

Your Top Five Self-Management Skills

Now go back through the lists of good-worker traits and self-management skills. Circle the five you feel are most important for an employer to know about you.

For each of these five skills, give a good example of when you used that skill. The examples can be from work, school, family experiences, or another type of life experience.

1. Skill: _____

    Example: _____

    _____

    _____

    _____

2. Skill: _____

    Example: _____

    _____

    _____

    _____

3. Skill: _____

    Example: _____

    _____

    _____

    _____

4. Skill: _____

   Example: _____

   _____

   _____

   _____

5. Skill: _____

   Example: _____

   _____

   _____

   _____

Activity

Identify Your Transferable Skills

As in the previous activity, check all the skills in the checklist that apply to you. Be sure you can prove them with specific examples.

Transferable Skills Checklist

Key Skills

These skills tend to get you higher levels of responsibility and pay. For this reason, they are worth emphasizing in interviews.

_____ Accept criticism

_____ Accept responsibility

_____ Communicate with others

_____ Complete assignments

_____ Cooperate with others/team player

_____ Instruct others

_____ Manage money

_____ Meet deadlines

_____ Solve problems

_____ Take pride in doing a good job

_____ Understand budgets

_____ Willing to learn

Other Transferable Skills

Using my hands/Dealing with things

_____ Assemble/build

_____ Construct/repair

_____ Drive/operate vehicles

_____ Follow safety procedures

_____ Good with hands

_____ Install/test

_____ Make new things

_____ Observe/inspect

_____ Operate tools, machines

_____ Use complex equipment

Dealing with data

_____ Calculate/compute numbers

_____ Check for accuracy/proofread

_____ Compare/compile data   _____ Observe/inspect

_____ Evaluate data   _____ Pay attention to details

_____ Keep financial records   _____ Record facts

_____ Locate information   _____ Research/investigate data

_____ Manage money   _____ Take inventory

Working with people

_____ Accept responsibility   _____ Instruct/teach others

_____ Comfort others   _____ Interview people

_____ Demonstrate   _____ Listen carefully

_____ Diplomatic/tactful   _____ Respect others

_____ Display leadership skills   _____ Sensitive/tolerant to others

_____ Help others   _____ Understand/trust others

Using words and ideas

_____ Articulate/speak clearly   _____ Edit

_____ Ask questions/inquire   _____ Follow directions

_____ Communicate verbally   _____ Remember information

_____ Correspond with others   _____ Use correct reasoning/logic

_____ Create new ideas   _____ Write clearly

(continues)

(continued)

Leadership

_____ Arrange social functions

_____ Compete against others

_____ Delegate duties   _____ Motivate people

_____ Direct others   _____ Plan activities

_____ Explain things to others _____ Run meetings

_____ Make decisions   _____ Solve problems

_____ Mediate problems   _____ Take risks

Dealing with technology

_____ Code, enter, and   _____ Perform basic
         debug programs   accounting tasks

_____ Design Web pages   _____ Perform desktop
                                           publishing functions
_____ Enter data
                                  _____ Perform word-processing
_____ Install/troubleshoot   functions
         programs
                                  _____ Use the Internet
_____ Operate computer systems
                                  _____ Use various software programs

Additional Transferable Skills

Add any transferable skills you have that are not in the list.

_____   _____

_____   _____

_____   _____

_____   _____

Your Top Five Transferable Skills

Now go back through the list of transferable skills. Circle the top five that you want to use in your next job. For each of these five skills, give a good example of when you used that skill.

1. Skill: _____

   Example: _____

   _____

   _____

2. Skill: _____

   Example: _____

   _____

   _____

3. Skill: _____

   Example: _____

   _____

   _____

4. Skill: _____

   Example: _____

   _____

   _____

5. Skill: _____

   Example: _____

   _____

   _____

Activity

Identify Your Job-Related Skills

Each job requires skills related to that particular job. Some job-related skills can be learned quickly, while others may take years of training. These skills are in addition to the self-management and transferable skills needed to succeed in that job.

Job-Related Skills Worksheet

Even if you have not yet worked in the job you want, you probably have some experience that relates to it.
This experience usually comes from several sources: courses you have taken; other jobs or volunteer work; and hobbies, family activities, and other experiences.

You should have some idea of the type of job you want. Even if you are not sure, write the title of a job that interests you here: _____

In the spaces below, list some job-related skills you have that fit this job.

1. Job-related skills you have gained from school courses or vocational training:

   _____

   _____

2. Job-related skills you have used in other work or volunteer experiences:

   _____

   _____

3. Job-related skills you have gained in hobbies, family activities, extracurricular activities, and other experiences outside of work or school:

   _____

   _____

CHAPTER 4

Documenting Your Education, Experience, and References

Telling an employer you can do a job is not enough. You have to prove you can do the job. You can do this by showing concrete examples of your experience and knowledge. These examples can come from many different areas including school, paid and unpaid work, hobbies, and everyday life. You also need references who can confirm your abilities and strengths.

Organize Your School and Work Background

The following activities will help you collect and organize information about your educational background, school experiences, training, honors, and hobbies. In addition, you will list your work experiences, including paid and unpaid jobs and volunteer work. In each activity, think about the points an employer might want to know about you. An example is your skills.

Remember that all jobs and experiences are valuable, no matter how little they paid or how small they seem. Employers are interested in what you can do. All experiences can help prove that you are a good worker.

Introducing the *Data Minder* Booklet

The activities that follow match the small, portable *Data Minder* booklet attached in the back of this workbook. You can use the *Data Minder* as your personal job search assistant. It is designed to help you remember the many details that you will need throughout your job search, such as dates, phone numbers, addresses, and information about your background.

You can carry the *Data Minder* with you once it is completed. Your *Data Minder* will help you do the following:

- ■ Remember key points covered throughout this course.

- ■ Fill out applications.

- ■ Write a resume.

- ■ Prepare for interviews.

Many activities contain page references to the *Data Minder* to help you easily transfer the information to the *Data Minder*. Follow your teacher's instructions in completing the *Data Minder*. Note that some of the *Data Minder* cannot be completed until you have covered material later in this workbook.

Activity

Your Educational Background

Data Minder page 3

List the schools you have attended in the following worksheet. Be sure to include your attendance dates.

Worksheet for Schools Attended

Grade	Dates	School Name	Address, City, State, Zip Code	Phone Number
12th				
11th				
10th				
9th				
8th				
7th				
6th				
5th				
4th				
3rd				
2nd				
1st				
Kindergarten				

Activity

Your High School Courses

Data Minder pages 4-5

A large part of your life experience comes from school. Since employers will be interested in this experience, use it to support your ability to do the job.

High School Classes Worksheet

1. What courses, including vocational courses, have you taken in high school?

   _____

   _____

   _____

   _____

2. What types of jobs might they prepare you for? _____

   _____

   _____

   _____

   _____

3. List the more important things you learned to do in these courses: _____

   _____

   _____

   _____

   _____

4. What tools and equipment did you learn to use?

_____

_____

_____

_____

5. How can you use these courses after you complete high school? _____

_____

_____

_____

_____

Activity

Your Extracurricular Activities

Data Minder page 5

Participation in sports, clubs, and other extracurricular activities can help show that you are a hard worker and have other skills.

List all the extracurricular activities that you have been involved in:

_____   _____

_____   _____

_____   _____

_____   _____

_____   _____

_____   _____

Select one activity you like most or that is most important to you, and complete the following worksheet. If you want to include more extracurricular activities, make copies of the worksheet or put the information on blank paper.

Extracurricular Activity Worksheet

1. Activity: _____

2. How many months or years involved? Give dates: _____

3. Leadership role(s) you held: _____

   _____

   _____

4. Describe what you did in this activity: _____

    _____

    _____

    _____

5. List any special achievements and honors: _____

    _____

    _____

6. List the self-management, transferable, and job-related skills used in this activity that would be important to a future employer:

_____   _____

_____   _____

_____   _____

_____   _____

_____   _____

Activity

Your Other Training

Data Minder page 6

List any formal or informal training you received that might help prepare you for a job, college, the military, and so on. Examples of such training are workshops, seminars, and self-study programs.

Other Training Worksheet

1. School or program name: _____

_____

2. Street address: _____

3. City, state, zip code: _____

4. Phone number: (   ) _____

5. Dates attended: _____

6. Type of education or training: _____

_____

_____

_____

7. Type of certification, degree, or special diploma: _____

_____

_____

_____

8. Job-related skills you learned:_____

_____

_____

_____

9. Tools, machinery, and equipment used in training: _____

_____

_____

_____

Activity

Your Work Experience

Data Minder pages 8-13

This activity collects information on jobs you have had. Include all part-time jobs, summer jobs, and internships here, even if you worked for a short time. Also use the worksheets for unpaid volunteer or informal work, such as helping in the family business, mowing lawns, baby-sitting, or similar activities. All of these things can count as "work." Start with the most recent job and work backward.

Volunteer/Paid Work Experience Worksheet

Job 1

1. Name of organization: _____

2. Street address: _____

3. City, state, zip code: _____

4. Phone number: (   ) _____

5. Supervisor or person in charge: _____

6. Job title: _____

7. Starting date: _____ Ending date: _____

8. Starting salary: _____ Ending salary: _____

9. List your job duties and responsibilities: _____

   _____

   _____

10. List raises or promotions you received: _____

    _____

11. Other recognition (such as positive evaluations)
    you received: _____

    _____

12. Reasons for leaving the job: _____

    _____

Job 2

1. Name of organization: _____

2. Street address: _____

3. City, state, zip code: _____

4. Phone number: (   ) _____

5. Supervisor or person in charge: _____

6. Job title: _____

7. Starting date: _____ Ending date: _____

8. Starting salary: _____ Ending salary: _____

9. List your job duties and responsibilities: _____

   _____

   _____

10. List raises or promotions you received: _____

    _____

11. Other recognition (such as positive evaluations) you received: _____

    _____

12. Reasons for leaving the job: _____

    _____

(continues)

(continued)

Job 3

1. Name of organization: _____

2. Street address: _____

3. City, state, zip code: _____

4. Phone number: (   ) _____

5. Supervisor or person in charge: _____

6. Job title: _____

7. Starting date: _____ Ending date: _____

8. Starting salary: _____ Ending salary: _____

9. List your job duties and responsibilities: _____

    _____

    _____

10. List raises or promotions you received: _____

    _____

11. Other recognition (such as positive evaluations) you received: _____

    _____

12. Reasons for leaving the job: _____

    _____

Job 4

1. Name of organization: _____

2. Street address: _____

3. City, state, zip code: _____

4. Phone number: (   ) _____

5. Supervisor or person in charge: _____

6. Job title: _____

7. Starting date: _____ Ending date: _____

8. Starting salary: _____ Ending salary: _____

9. List your job duties and responsibilities: _____

_____

_____

10. List raises or promotions you received: _____

_____

11. Other recognition (such as positive evaluations) you received: _____

_____

12. Reasons for leaving the job: _____

_____

Job 5

1. Name of organization: _____

2. Street address: _____

3. City, state, zip code: _____

4. Phone number: (   ) _____

5. Supervisor or person in charge: _____

6. Job title: _____

7. Starting date: _____ Ending date: _____

8. Starting salary: _____ Ending salary: _____

(continues)

(continued)

9. List your job duties and responsibilities: _____

_____

_____

10. List raises or promotions you received: _____

_____

11. Other recognition (such as positive evaluations) you received: _____

_____

12. Reasons for leaving the job: _____

_____

Job 6

1. Name of organization: _____

2. Street address: _____

3. City, state, zip code: _____

4. Phone number: (   ) _____

5. Supervisor or person in charge: _____

6. Job title: _____

7. Starting date: _____ Ending date: _____

8. Starting salary: _____ Ending salary: _____

9. List your job duties and responsibilities: _____

_____

_____

10. List raises or promotions you received: _____

_____

11. Other recognition (such as positive evaluations) you
    received: _____

    _____

12. Reasons for leaving the job: _____

    _____

Activity

Your Professional Memberships, Hobbies, Honors, and Family Responsibilities

Data Minder pages 14-15

The activities you do outside of school and at home show that you have experience or a special interest in something. The same is true of awards and honors you've received.

You may not think that some of these activities can count as experience, but many employers consider them. These activities can be even more important if you have little paid work experience.

Think about the things you have done outside of school and at home that required responsibility, hard work, or special knowledge, or that you feel you did well. Also think about any awards or honors you've received.

Other Experiences Worksheet

1. **Professional memberships.** This includes memberships related to a job (such as a grocery store union) or chosen career field (such as the Future Teacher's Association). Be sure to list any leadership roles you held. _____

   _____

   _____

   _____

   _____

2. **Hobbies.** Give details about each hobby, emphasizing skills and accomplishments: _____

   _____

   _____

_____

_____

_____

_____

3. **Honors, awards, achievements.** Give details, including dates: _____

_____

_____

_____

_____

_____

_____

4. **Family responsibilities.** Give details and emphasize responsibilities and skills
   you used or learned: _____

_____

_____

_____

_____

_____

_____

Select Your References

Many employers want to verify the points you have told them about yourself. They will ask you for the names of people who know you and your work. Here are the sources of the most common references.

Work References

These are people who can tell employers that you are likely to make a good worker. The best work references are usually the people who supervised you on paid or volunteer jobs. Other good choices are older coworkers, teachers, coaches, and leaders of any social or religious groups who know what kind of work you do. Most employers think that these are the best sources of information for determining the kind of worker you are.

Personal References

Personal references are people who know what you are like as a person and who have known you for at least two years. Most employers will not bother to contact a relative or friend about you. They know that these people like you but may not be able to give them information about your work skills. The best personal references include adult friends of your family, parents of your best friends, neighbors, and clergy.

Be sure to ask people if you may use them as references during your job search.

Tips for Listing Your References

Element	Example
Reference's full name	Mr./Mrs./Miss/Ms.
Job title or relationship to you	Vocational Instructor
Place of employment	Local School
Street address	500 N. Gulf Road
City, state, zip code	Anytown, Georgia 00001
Area code and home or work phone number	Work: (555) 555-0000
E-mail address (if available)	teacher@email.com

- Always ask people if you can use them as references first and discuss what they will say about you.

- Tell them the type of job you are looking for and the skills and experience you have to do it well.

- Be sure to list four or five people who will say only good things about you.

- Include both work and personal references.

- Do not use any relatives or friends as references.

- Make sure your references can be reached easily by phone during the day. This is when most employers will call.

- Create a one-page list of references as shown in the example on the next page.

Sample References

REFERENCES

for

ROBERT B. HIRED

Center each reference ———

Mr. William Jones
Criminal Justice Instructor
Neighborhood Vocational School
7300 North Palmyra Road
Anytown, Ohio 00001
Work: (555) 555-1111

Rev. Frederick Smith
Pastor
Neighborhood Lutheran Church
745 Market Street
Anytown, Ohio 00001
Home: (555) 555-2222

Include about four
references—both
work and personal

Separate each
——— reference with two
or three blank lines

Mr. George Thomas
Guidance Counselor
Neighborhood High School
500 Educational Highway
Anytown, Ohio 00001
Work: (555) 555-3333
gthomas@dot.com

Mrs. Jane Doe
Office Manager
Steel Valley Crane Company
42 Main Street
Anytown, Ohio 00001
Work: (555) 555-4444
Home: (555) 555-5555
steelvalley@net.com

Do not number references

Activity

Gather Information on Your References

Data Minder pages 16-19

In the spaces below, list the persons you might use as your work and personal references.

Work References Worksheet

Name: _____

Job title: _____

Place of employment: _____

Street address: _____

City, state, zip code: _____

Phone number: (   ) _____

E-mail address: _____

Name: _____

Job title: _____

Place of employment: _____

Street address: _____

City, state, zip code: _____

Phone number: (   ) _____

E-mail address: _____

(continues)

(continued)

Name: _____

Job title: _____

Place of employment: _____

Street address: _____

City, state, zip code: _____

Phone number: (   ) _____

E-mail address: _____

Name: _____

Job title: _____

Place of employment: _____

Street address: _____

City, state, zip code: _____

Phone number: (   ) _____

E-mail address: _____

Personal References Worksheet

Name: _____

Relationship: _____

Place of employment: _____

Street address: _____

City, state, zip code: _____

Phone number: (   ) _____

E-mail address: _____

Name: _____

Relationship: _____

Place of employment: _____

Street address: _____

City, state, zip code: _____

Phone number: (   ) _____

E-mail address: _____

Name: _____

Relationship: _____

Place of employment: _____

Street address: _____

City, state, zip code: _____

Phone number: (   ) _____

E-mail address: _____

Name: _____

Position: _____

Place of employment: _____

Street address: _____

City, state, zip code: _____

Phone number: (   ) _____

E-mail address: _____

Use This Information to Your Advantage

As you will learn in Chapter 11, you have only a few minutes to make a good impression in an interview. You will have to tell employers about the skills and experiences that make you a good person for the job. This makes it important that you know, in advance, the most important details to tell employers about yourself. You probably have more positive things to tell them than you realized. We hope this chapter helped.

CHAPTER 5

The JIST Card® — A Mini-Resume

A JIST Card is a mini-resume that can be used in many ways during your job search. In this chapter, you will learn how to write and use a JIST Card effectively.

Basic Information About You

Although a JIST Card is only three-by-five inches, it will include the information most employers need to know about you.

Read the sample JIST Card below. Imagine that you are an employer who hires people with similar skills. Your "company" may or may not have a job opening at this time. Review the information on the card and let yourself react naturally to what you feel about this potential employee:

John Kijek
Home: (876) 232-9213
Pager: (876) 637-6643
E-mail: jkijek@net.com

Position Desired: Administrative Assistant

Skills: Over two years' work experience, including one year in a full-time training program. Familiar with spreadsheet programs, database programs, computerized accounting systems, Internet use, and most standard computer operations. Word process at 55 wpm using good format and grammar. Have trained three staff members in a retail environment and helped increase sales more than 12%. Good writing and language skills. I work well independently and as part of a team.

Will relocate.

Honest, reliable, hard working, and well organized.

What Do You Think About the JIST Card?

1. If you were an employer, how would you feel about the person whose JIST Card you just read? _____

   _____

   _____

   _____

   _____

   _____

   _____

2. Would you interview this person if you had an opening? _____

Although JIST Cards appear to give very little information, most employers feel positive about them. Many employers would give this applicant an interview if they had an opening. They are that impressed!

TIP

In Chapter 3, you identified the self-management, transferable, and job-related skills that you felt were most important for a job, and you supported each skill with an example. These skills and examples will be used in developing your own JIST Card.

Some Ways You Can Use a JIST Card

- Attach one to your application or resume.
- Present one as your business card before or after an interview.
- Leave one or more with your references.
- Give several to each of your friends, relatives, and others who might help you in your job search. Ask them to pass your JIST Card on to others who might know of an opening.

- Leave one with employers when you are refused an application or an interview. (It could help them change their minds!)
- Enclose one in a thank-you note following an interview or with other job search correspondence.

Write any other ideas for the use of your JIST Card here:

_____

_____

_____

_____

_____

_____

Anatomy of a JIST Card

JIST Cards are more complicated than they first appear. Look over the various parts of a JIST Card in the following sample. It will help you learn how to create your own card.

John Kijek —— Name
Home: (876) 232-9213 —— 2 phone numbers
Pager: (876) 637-6643
E-mail: jkijek@net.com —— E-mail address

Position Desired: Administrative Assistant —— Position

Experience, education, and training

Skills: Over two years' work experience, including one year in a full-time training program. Familiar with spreadsheet programs, database programs, computerized accounting systems, Internet use, and most standard computer operations. Word process at 55 wpm using good format and grammar. Have trained three staff members in a retail environment and helped increase sales more than 12%. Good writing and language skills. I work well independently and as part of a team.

Job-related skills and results

Transferable skills

Will relocate. —— Special conditions

Honest, reliable, hard working, and well organized. —— Good-worker traits and self-management skills

---

3-x-5 white or light-color card

Tips for Writing Your JIST Card

- **Name.** Use your name as it is spoken. Avoid nicknames.

- **Phone number.** An employer will most likely contact you by phone or e-mail. If your home phone is not always answered during the day (or if you don't have a phone), ask a reliable friend or relative to take messages. Another option is to get voicemail or an answering machine. Just make sure your message sounds professional. Many JIST Cards include a second phone number to increase the chance of an employer reaching you. This may be a pager number, a cell phone number, or some other alternate phone number.

- **E-mail address.** Include your e-mail address if you have one. Keep in mind that free e-mail accounts are available through a variety of sources. If you don't have a computer, you can access your account at libraries and schools with Internet connections.

Use an objective that allows you to be considered for several jobs.

- **Position/job objective.** If your job objective is too specific, it will limit the jobs for which you may be considered. Instead, use a job objective that allows you to be considered for more positions, yet is not too general.

- **Skills.** Skills can be reflected in several ways:

  - ✔ **Education and experience.** Take credit for everything you've done. Everything can count, including education, training, paid employment, related volunteer work, hobbies, and other informal experience. Use the following formula to figure your total length of experience. Then list your total experience:

Experience	Months/Years
1. Total time worked in similar jobs	
2. Total time worked in other jobs	
3. Total time informal experience, volunteer work, and related hobbies	
4. Total time in related training and education	
Total Experience/Time (add 1 + 2 + 3 + 4)	

✔ **Job-related skills and results.** Mention the things you can do specific to the job, such as using special tools or computers. Emphasize accomplishments and use numbers (such as percentage of sales or profits increased, number of units produced, and so on).

✔ **Transferable skills.** Mention ones that are important to the job and that you do well. Refer to the skills checklists in Chapter 3. Use examples where possible.

✔ **Self-management skills.** Include at least three of your strongest self-management skills. Select the ones from your checklist in Chapter 3 that seem important for this job.

● **Special conditions.** This is an optional section. Use it to list special advantages you offer that don't fit elsewhere.

Sample JIST Cards

Look over the sample JIST Cards that follow for ideas for your own.

Jonn Scott
Home: (219) 298-9704
E-mail: jscott@hotmail.com

Position: Retail Sales

Two years' work experience plus two years' education in distributive education and marketing. Experience in fast-paced environment serving as many as 1,200 customers a day with weekly sales of over $24,000. Familiar with retail display, purchasing, sales recording, selling techniques, and supervision of others. Excellent interpersonal and customer service skills.

Available full time. Will work weekends and evenings.

Results oriented, reliable, professional.

Note: Jonn's work experience was at a McDonald's and a senior-year co-op job. His education was in his high school business program.

Lisa Marie Marrin

Home: (213) 432-8064   Pager: (212) 876-9487

Position: Hotel Management

Two years of experience in sales, customer service, and catering for a 300-room hotel. Courses in business, marketing, computer skills, and distributive education. Organized catering events for groups as large as 200 and suggested improvements in registration procedures that saved over $10,000 a year in personnel costs. Have been commended for improving staff productivity and courtesy. I approach my work with industry, imagination, and creative problem-solving skills.

Prefer full-time work with promotion potential.

Enthusiastic, well organized, detail oriented.

Note: Lisa Marie had worked for the hotel on weekends and during summers while going to high school. She took several business and computer courses and plans to continue to work in the hospitality industry to pay her way through college.

Richard Straightarrow

Message: (602) 257-6643   E-mail: richthearrow@arrow.net

Objective: Computer support specialist or Internet site developer

One year of work experience plus extensive knowledge of computer hardware and software. Can troubleshoot and repair all major PC computers and peripherals, including business "rack" systems. Familiar with many software packages, including major word processing, database, spreadsheet, graphic design, and utility programs. Have set up, updated, trained, and supported many new and experienced PC users. Have also designed and managed over 10 Web sites, the largest with over 2,000 pages and 800,000 hits a year. Efficient at managing many priorities and heavy workloads.

Willing to work long hours in an informal work environment.

Good people skills, learn quickly, reliable.

Note: Richard's computer skills are all self-taught. He has been into computers for years and spends much of his free time working with hardware and software and with other computer enthusiasts. He has earned enough from his freelance Web design work to buy his car and save for more formal education.

Sandy Zaremba Home: (512) 232-7608
Message: (512) 234-7465

Position: General Office/Clerical

Over one-and-a-half years of work experience, plus one year of training in office practices. Type 55 wpm, trained in word-processing operations, post general ledger, handle payables, receivables, and most computerized accounting tasks. Good interpersonal skills and get along with most people. Can meet deadlines and handle pressure well.

Willing to work any hours.

Organized, honest, reliable, and hard working.

Note: Sandy got her experience as a volunteer in her church business office and after school in a small bookkeeping firm. She also took some high school computer and office skills classes.

Maria Smith **Home:** (888) 9999
E-mail: msmith@mail.com

Position: Office support staff

Qualifications: Graduating from high school in June XXXX. Focused on academic and business courses, including accounting, keyboarding, computer literacy, and exploratory business. Able to produce various office documents. Capable of using personal computer, transcriber, and software such as Microsoft Office, PageMaker, and Web browsers. Proficient in keeping records and in using correct grammar, spelling, and punctuation. Efficient in following instructions and meeting deadlines.

Available for part-time work, weekdays after noon.

Organized — Dependable — Accurate — Professional

Note: Maria will be graduating from high school in less than a year. While she has not had formal work experience, her high school business courses and self-taught software skills make her marketable for a good part-time job now.

Activity

Your Practice JIST Card

Use the following worksheet to write a first draft of your JIST Card. You may want to make rough drafts of some sections on separate sheets of paper. When your information is right, you can then transfer it to this worksheet.

JIST Card First Draft Worksheet

Name: _____

Home phone number: _____

Alternate phone number: _____

E-mail address: _____

Position desired: _____

_____

Education and training: _____

_____

_____

_____

_____

Job-related experience: _____

_____

_____

_____

_____

© JIST Works, Inc., Indianapolis, IN

Job-related skills and results statement:

_____

_____

_____

_____

Transferable skills statement: _____

_____

_____

_____

_____

_____

Special conditions (optional): _____

_____

_____

_____

Good-worker traits and self-management skills: _____

_____

_____

_____

_____

_____

_____

Activity

Your Final JIST Card

Data Minder pages 20-21

Now use the information from the worksheet you just completed to write your JIST Card in the spaces that follow. Modify the words below as needed.

JIST Card Final Draft Worksheet

(Name:) _____

Home phone number: _____

Alternate phone number: _____

E-mail address: _____

Position desired: _____

Experience, education, and training

_____

Skills: Over _____ months/years of experience in _____ , plus

training/courses in _____ and _____ .

Skilled in _____ , _____ , _____ , _____ , _____ .

Able to _____ , _____ , _____ , _____ and _____

10-12 job-related skills and results

I have done _____ , _____ , _____ and _____ .

2 transferable skills

I am also _____ and _____ .

Available: _____ .

_____ , _____ , _____ , _____ .

4 self-management skills

Special conditions

© JIST Works, Inc., Indianapolis, IN

Tips for Producing Your JIST Card

- Make sure your JIST Card has no grammar or spelling errors. Check those phone numbers and e-mail addresses for accuracy.

- Make arrangements to have your card professionally produced on index (heavy) weight paper. A good-quality photocopy machine can often give you what you need. You can also create and print out your cards on a personal computer and laser printer.

- Discuss different ways to format your card. Experiment, be creative, and make yours look attractive and professional.

- Consider using a soft, light paper color, such as white, ivory, beige, cream, or gray.

- Most JIST cards are approximately three-by-five inches, but you can be a bit creative with yours if you want to. Some people have used a business-card size or a folded card to make theirs stand out.

- Be sure to see and approve the final draft before the printer completes your order.

- Print at least 50 to 100 cards, so you can give them out freely to employers and people you know.

JIST Cards can be very effective in helping you find job leads. But they won't work unless you use them. So plan on getting as many into the hands of employers, friends, relatives, and others as soon as you can.

CHAPTER 6

Finding Job Leads

For some people, finding *a* job is not too hard. Many young people can find entry-level jobs (in restaurants and fast-food places, for example) quite easily. But finding a really good job is often more difficult. The competition is greater. More people with more education, training, or experience are applying for the desirable jobs. This chapter covers various job search techniques that will give you the competitive edge in getting both entry-level and career-oriented jobs.

Most employers hire people they already know.

Activity

How Do People Find Jobs?

The major techniques people use to find jobs are listed below. Write the percentage of job seekers you think actually found jobs using each technique. The total should equal 100 percent.

1. Found a lead in the help-wanted ads. _____

2. Heard about the opening from people they knew. _____

3. Referred by state or private employment service. _____

4. Contacted the employer directly. _____

5. Referred by school placement office. _____

6. Took the civil service test. _____

7. Used other methods, including the Internet. _____

Total _____ 100% _____

Compare your guesses with others in the class, and then look up the answers at the end of this chapter. Discuss your guesses and the actual figures in class.

Where to Find Job Leads

Most people are surprised to find that fewer than 15 percent of all job seekers get their jobs from reading the want ads. The Internet also lists many job openings. But like the want ads, only a small percentage of all openings is listed there.

Many employers don't advertise at all. They hire people they already know. In fact, most people get jobs using other, informal job search methods like networking and making cold calls to employers. This is how job seekers find the "hidden" job market.

The chart below shows how people actually find jobs. Notice that about two-thirds of all job seekers get their jobs using informal methods, which are explained in the next sections.

How People Find Jobs

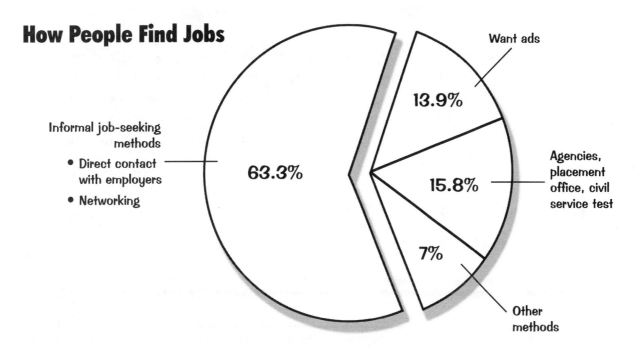

Informal job-seeking methods
- Direct contact with employers
- Networking

63.3%

Want ads

13.9%

Agencies, placement office, civil service test

15.8%

7%

Other methods

Informal Job Search Methods

The two basic informal job search methods are *networking* with people you know (warm contacts) and making direct contacts with employers (cold contacts). Both methods are based on the most important job search rule of all:

Don't wait until the job is open!

Most jobs get filled by someone the employer meets before a job is formally open. So the trick is to meet people who can hire you *before* a job is available! Instead of saying "Do you have any job openings?" say "I realize you may not have any openings now, but I would still like to talk to you about the possibility of future openings."

Networking with Warm Contacts: The Most Effective Job Search Method

Many job seekers find their jobs through leads provided by friends, relatives, and acquaintances. We call these people *warm contacts* because they know you and are the ones most likely to help. Contacting these people is the most effective job search method for most job seekers. Developing new contacts is called networking. The next activity shows you how it works.

Activity

Establish Warm Contacts

1. **Develop a list of all the groups of people you know.** Begin with your friends and relatives. Then think of other groups of people with whom you have something in common. Examples are people you used to work with, people who went to your school, people in your social or sports groups, former employers, friends' parents, and members of your religious group.

Groups of People You Know Worksheet

Group	Number of People in This Group
Friends	
Relatives	

2. **Develop a separate list of the people you know in each group.** Some lists, such as a list of your friends, may be quite long. For other lists, you may not know the names of everyone in the group. Examples are all the people who go to your church or people who graduated from your school in years past. You can get these names later. Just keep in mind that almost all these people will be willing to help you in your job search.

The worksheet that follows will help you list the people from two of your groups in an organized way. Complete this worksheet for two groups you listed, and use additional sheets for other groups. We suggest that you begin by listing your friends and relatives.

Network Contact Worksheet

Group 1

Name	Phone Number

(continues)

(continued)

Group 2	
Name	**Phone Number**

3. **Contact people.** Start with your friends and relatives. Call them and explain that you are looking for a job and need their help. Be as clear as possible about what you are looking for and about your skills and qualifications. Look at your JIST Card from Chapter 5 and the phone script in Chapter 7 for presentation ideas.

4. **Ask for leads.** Some of the people you contact may know of a job opening just right for you. If so, get the details and get right on it! More than likely, however, they will not know of an opening, so here are three questions you should ask.

The Three Magic Questions

- Do you know of any employers who may have an opening for someone with my skills? If no, then ask:

- Do you know of someone else who might know of such an opening? If yes, get that person's name and phone number and ask for another name. If no, then ask:

- Do you know someone who knows lots of people? If all else fails, this will usually get you a name.

5. **Keep records.** Keep a record of all your contacts. Simple three-by-five-inch index cards are very useful for recording important information, and they are easy to organize. Use the following example as a model.

Job Lead Card

Organization: **Mutual Health Insurance**

Contact person: **Anna Tomey**

Phone number: **(555) 555-2211**

Source of lead: **Aunt Ruth**

Notes: 4/10 called. Anna on vacation. Call back 4/15. 4/15 Interview set 4/20 at 1:30. 4/20 Anna showed me around. They use the same computers we used in school. Sent thank-you note and JIST Card. Call back 5/1. 5/1 Second interview 5/8 at 9 a.m.

6. **Follow up.** Call the people your contacts suggest and repeat steps 3, 4, and 5. For each original contact, you can extend your network of acquaintances by hundreds of people. It will be like the following illustration. Eventually, one of these people will hire you or refer you to someone who will!

Networking: One Person Refers You to Two Others

Tips for Following Up on Network Contacts

■ Keep a record of all your contacts.

■ Always complete a follow-up card for each contact.

■ Have plenty of index cards on hand.

■ Be pleasant and professional in all contacts.

■ Within 24 hours, send a thank-you note to each person you contact.

■ Include a copy of your JIST Card in all correspondence.

■ Get a card file box (available at office-supply stores), and file your job lead cards under the date you want to follow up.

Cold Contacts: Contacting Employers Directly

It takes more courage, but contacting an employer directly is a very effective job search technique. Since most jobs are not advertised, one effective way to find openings is to call employers who might need a person with your skills. The yellow pages is a very good source of places to call. Another source is the Internet, which provides a variety of ways to find places to call. For example, yellow pages listings are available online for any geographic area of the country. Many businesses have Web sites that provide company information and contact numbers.

Also, America's Career InfoNet at www.acinet.org is sponsored by the U.S. government and gives contact information for individual employers. Employers are organized by industry and location.

Once you locate an organization that may need your skills, give the company a call. Simply ask for the person in charge and ask if you can come in for an interview. You will learn more about how to do this later in this workbook.

You can also just walk in and ask to speak to the person in charge. This is particularly effective in small businesses but works surprisingly well in larger ones too. Remember, you want an interview even if no openings exist now.

Contacting an employer directly is a very effective job search technique.

TIP

If your timing is inconvenient, ask for a better time to come back for an interview. It works!

Pay Attention to Small Businesses

About two out of three people now work in smaller businesses—those with 250 or fewer workers. While the largest corporations have reduced their number of employees, small businesses have been creating as many as 80 percent of all new jobs. Many opportunities exist to obtain training and to advance in smaller organizations too. Many do not even have personnel departments, so nontraditional job search techniques are particularly effective with them.

Where People Work

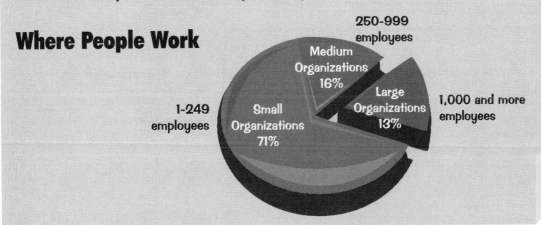

250-999 employees

Medium Organizations 16%

Large Organizations 13%

1,000 and more employees

1-249 employees

Small Organizations 71%

Activity

Use the Yellow Pages

1. Find the index section in the current yellow pages. This is usually in the front of the book. It lists the various types of businesses and other organizations within each area. (If you do not have a complete copy of the local yellow pages, look at the sample page from another city's yellow pages on the next page. Your instructor will tell you what to do.)

2. Begin looking at the listings and ask yourself this question: "Could this type of organization possibly use a person with my skills?" (It will help if you have a job objective here, such as "administrative assistant" or "auto mechanic.")

3. List at least 10 types of organizations from the yellow pages index that might hire people with your skills. Record these 10 types of organizations on the worksheet that follows. For each organization, list the page number in the yellow pages where you could look up more information.

Yellow Pages Worksheet 1: Types of Organizations

Type of Organization	Page Number in Yellow Pages
1.	
2.	
3.	
4.	
5.	

Type of Organization	Page Number in Yellow Pages
6.	
7.	
8.	
9.	
10.	

(continues)

(continued)

Continue looking at every listing in the yellow pages index. This will help you discover many employers that you would normally overlook. For each listing, ask the same question:

Could this type of organization possibly use a person with my skills?

When the answer is "yes," decide how interested you are in working for this type of organization and mark the entry with one of the following codes:

- 1 = Very interested
- 2 = Somewhat interested
- 3 = Not interested

Go back and put a 1, 2, or 3 by each of the 10 types of organizations you listed in the worksheet you just completed.

List Specific Organizations

Next turn to the yellow pages section for each type of organization and list the specific companies or organizations there. These organizations are hot prospects for you to contact in your job search. The Yellow Pages Worksheet 2 gives you an example of how the contact information can be organized. Make copies of the worksheet as needed.

In Chapter 7, you will learn how to contact each organization and ask for an interview. In this way you can generate many job leads from the hidden job market.

Yellow Pages Worksheet 2: Specific Organizations

Group 1. Yellow Pages Index Listing:		Group 2. Yellow Pages Index Listing:	
Specific Organization	Phone Number	Specific Organization	Phone Number

TIP

For each contact, follow up with a thank-you note and include your JIST Card.

Traditional Job Search Methods

While informal job search methods are more effective for most people, you may want to use some of the more traditional methods as well. Here is information on the major traditional methods you may wish to try:

- **Respond to help-wanted ads.** As you already know, most jobs are not advertised. And there are problems even with those that are! Everyone who reads the paper or finds them on the Internet knows about those job openings. As a result, the competition for these jobs will often be fierce. Still, some people do get jobs this way, so go ahead and apply. Just be sure to spend most of your time using more effective methods.

- **Use the state employment service.** Often called the unemployment office, this service offers free job leads. But the office is likely to know of only 10 percent or less of the available jobs in your area. However, it is worth a weekly visit. If you ask for the same counselor, you might impress him or her enough to remember you and refer the better openings to you.

  If you have Internet access, you can find employment service job postings for any state at www.ajb.dni.us.

- **Use your school placement office.** Staff members can provide job leads and give job counseling.

- **Use private employment agencies.** These for-profit businesses charge a fee either to you (as high as 20 percent of your annual salary!) or the employer. They find most job leads by calling employers. This is a technique you will learn to do yourself. Unless you have skills that are in high demand, you will probably do better on your own—and save money, too.

- **Send out resumes.** Sending resumes to people you don't know does not work well for most people. A much better approach is to phone the person who might hire you in order to set up an interview directly, and then send a resume. Tips on resume writing and using resumes appear in Chapter 9.

- **Fill out applications.** Because of the shortage of workers for entry-level jobs, filling out applications is more effective for young people than for more experienced workers. While many organizations may require an application, remember that your task is to get an interview, not to fill out an application. When you do need to complete an application, make it neat and error free, and do not include anything that could get you screened out. If necessary, leave a problem section blank. You can always explain it after you get an offer. Tips on completing applications appear in Chapter 10.

- **Contact personnel departments.** Few people get hired by someone in a personnel department. The personnel department's job is to screen you out. Be cooperative with personnel staff, but try to go directly to the person who is most likely to supervise you, even if no opening exists just now. Remember that most smaller organizations don't even have a personnel office—only the larger ones do.

- **Apply at temporary agencies.** Temporary employment agencies can place you on temporary job assignments. As long as you don't pay a fee, this can be a good and quick way to get a job. A temporary job will help you learn about different work environments and gain new skills. Many temp workers get job offers from employers who like their work.

Use the Internet for Job Leads

The Internet is becoming an increasingly important source of job leads. This is especially true for technical and in-demand positions. While informal methods still work best for finding job leads, you may wish to explore some of the following:

- **Resume banks.** These sites collect resumes and make them accessible to employers. One such site is at www.monster.com. One drawback to resume banks is that many job seekers assume they can simply put resumes in Internet resume databanks, and employers will line up to hire them. It sometimes happen this way, but not often. This is the same negative experience that people have when sending lots of unsolicited resumes to personnel offices—a hopeful but mostly ineffective approach that has been around long before computers.

  While people are getting jobs through the Internet, it is still essential that you take an active rather than a passive approach in your job search. This is especially true when you are looking for local, part-time, and entry-level jobs.

- **Company Web sites.** Many companies post job openings on their Web sites. Again, this may be a good source of leads for some people. Keep in mind that many job seekers are seeing these same listings, and competition can be great. One big value of company Web sites is as a research tool to help you prepare for interviews and find out about a company's mission and products.

- **Internet service providers and Web portals.** Providers such as America Online and Web portals such as Yahoo! offer many career resources and links.

- **JIST's Web site.** You can go to www.jist.com to get links to career sites and other helpful information.

- **America's Career InfoNet.** The government-sponsored site at www.acinet.org is a comprehensive source of occupational and employer information.

> You could spend weeks and months browsing the Internet. Your task is to get a job, not to wander the Web endlessly.

Answers to "How Do People Find Jobs?"

Some job search techniques are more effective than others. The following figures show the percentage of people who got their jobs by using the various job search techniques. These are the correct answers to the first activity in this chapter. How close were your answers?

1. 13.9 percent answered help-wanted ads.

2. 28.4 percent heard about an opening from people they knew.

3. 10.7 percent were referred by a state employment service or a private employment agency.

4. 34.9 percent contacted employers directly.

5. 3 percent were referred by a school placement office.

6. 2.1 percent took civil service tests.

7. 7 percent used other miscellaneous methods, including getting leads from the Internet, through a union hiring hall, by placing journal ads, and so on.

CHAPTER 7

Contacting Employers by Phone and in Person

Remember that most jobs are never advertised. They are found in the hidden job market. As explained in Chapter 6, making cold contacts with employers is a very effective way to find these hidden jobs. You can make these cold contacts with employers by

- Calling them on the phone.
- Visiting them in person.

This chapter discusses calling employers on the phone, and then shows how to adapt this technique to visiting employers in person. Both methods are considered cold contacts because you do not know the employers.

Contact Employers by Telephone

Using the telephone in your job search offers many advantages:

- **Saves time and money.** Most people can call 10 to 20 employers in one hour. You might spend a whole day contacting the same number of employers in person. You also save transportation money and related costs.

- **Creates new opportunities.** By calling potential employers directly, you can often uncover job openings long before they will be advertised. An employer may even create a job for you because you sound like the right person with the right skills.

- **Makes a positive impression.** Good telephone skills can create a positive impression. This will give you the edge over those who simply fill out an application or send in a resume. You also appear more assertive.

- **Gets directly to the hiring authority.** Using the phone makes it much easier to get directly to the person who is most likely to supervise someone with your skills. It is much more effective than filling out applications or sending in resumes.

- **Gets results.** People who use the telephone well can get many more interviews than people using traditional methods. Many will also get job offers sooner.

You Can Do It!

Many people find it hard to make phone calls to employers they don't know. They are afraid of being rejected. But preparation can make it much easier. The two most important things to do are the following:

- Know what you are going to say in advance.

- Practice your telephone presentation by yourself and with others until you feel prepared to make calls to employers.

A Sample Telephone Script

Your JIST Card, with just a few changes, can form the basis for an effective telephone script. Here is an example based on a JIST Card presented in Chapter 5:

May I speak to the person in charge of your business office?

Hello, my name is Maria Smith, and I'm interested in office support work. I'll be graduating from high school in June and have been focusing on academic and business courses, including accounting, keyboarding, computer literacy, and exploratory business. From these courses, I have hands-on experience in producing various office documents and doing basic accounting tasks, including spreadsheets.

I can keep accurate records, and I am familiar with various software, including Microsoft Office, PageMaker, and Web browsers. I think you will find me to be very organized, dependable, and professional.

When may I come in for an interview?

How Does It Sound to You?

If you were an employer, how would you feel about someone saying the sample script to you on the phone? Would you give this person an interview?

The telephone script based on your JIST Card is a powerful tool.

When asked this same question, most employers say they would interview this person. They were interested enough in what the person said to consider her for an opening—even if they did not have one right away! From beginning to end, this phone script takes less than 30 seconds to say out loud. Yet many employers have granted interviews on just this much information.

The Six Parts of a Telephone Script

A telephone script has six basic parts, as listed below:

Part of Phone Script	What It Is
1. The target	The person who would supervise you
2. The name	Who you are
3. The job	What you want to do
4. The hook	What you have to offer
5. The goal	To get an interview or a referral
6. The closing	Saying thank you and goodbye

Here are more details on each part of a phone script:

1. **The target:** Do not ask for the personnel department. Instead, ask for the department where you would like to work. *May I please speak to the person in charge of the* _____ *department.*

2. **The name:** Give the employer your first and last name here, just like you would if you were introducing yourself in person.

   Hello, my name is _____ .

3. **The job:** Give the job title or type of job you want here. *I am interested in a position as a* _____ .

4. **The hook:** Include details from the skills section of your JIST Card here.

   Example: *I'll be graduating in June from a two-year vocational program in* _____ _____ *, which included hands-on training. I've also taken* _____ (one semester, one year, two years, and so on) *of high school* _____ .

   I have _____ (months/years) *of* _____

   (various, other, or related) *job experience. Some of my skills include* _____

   _____

   (state three to five of your most impressive job-related or lab skills—tasks you already know how to do well).

5. **The goal:** *When may I come in for an interview?*

   ● If you get an interview: *Great. I'm really interested in talking with you about this position. When would be a good time?* If you don't get an interview for a job that is open now, ask for an interview to discuss future openings and to learn more about the company.

   ● If you don't get an interview, ask all of the following: (a) *May I call you back about possible openings in the near future?* (b) *May I send you a resume?* and (c) *Do you know of anyone else I might contact?*

6. **The closing:** *Thank you very much for your time. I'll see you on* _____ (date and time) *for my interview.*

Activity

Prepare Your Telephone Script

Each part of the phone script is covered in the following worksheet. Use the information from your JIST Card to fill out each section. Because people speak differently than they write, change the content of your JIST Card so that it sounds natural when spoken.

Before you complete the worksheet, use separate sheets of paper to create a rough draft of each worksheet section. Edit your material until it sounds good enough to write on the worksheet. You will write your complete, final telephone script at the end of the chapter.

Telephone Contact Worksheet

1. **The target:** *May I please speak to the person in charge of the* _____ *department?*

2. **The name:** *Hello, my name is* _____ .

3. **The job:** *I am interested in a position as a* _____ .

4. **The hook:** Include details from the skills section of your JIST Card here.

   _____

   _____

   _____

5. **The goal:** *When may I come in for an interview?* If you are unable to get an interview, ask if you can call back and send a resume. Ask if the employer knows of any other organizations that would need someone with your skills.

6. **The closing:** *Thank you very much for your time. I'll see you on* _____ *(date and time) for my interview.*

Practice Your Phone Script!

Keep rewriting your telephone script until it sounds right. The first five parts of the final version should take you between 25 and 30 seconds to read aloud in a conversational style. Rehearse it several times. Practice speaking distinctly, clearly, and with expression so it sounds like normal conversation and not a written speech.

Reminders for Contacting Employers by Phone

- **Get through to the hiring authority,** the one person most likely to supervise you.

- **Present your entire script.** Do this clearly and without interruption.

- **Get an interview.** Be prepared to ask for an interview...
  - ✔ For the position you want. *If no, then...*
  - ✔ To discuss future openings. *If no, then...*
  - ✔ For information about the organization.

- **If you do not get an interview:**
  - ✔ Set up a date and time to call back.
  - ✔ Ask if you can send a resume.
  - ✔ Get a referral.

Overcome Typical Problems When Calling Employers

You now have a draft script to use in your phone calls. When you make your phone calls, you need to be prepared to handle several common problems. Here are some examples:

- How do you get past the operator, receptionist, or assistant who is trained to screen calls such as the one you are making?

- How do you get around voicemail to reach the person in charge?

- How do you respond to "Sorry, there are no openings"?

- How do you avoid an interview over the phone?

These are just a few of the situations that you may encounter as you make your telephone contacts. To overcome them, you need to have clear objectives and know a few helpful techniques.

Notice how the following common situations are handled. Do the sample responses meet the goals of a telephone contact?

Situation 1: You ask to speak to the manager, supervisor, or director in charge of the job you are seeking. You do not want to get referred to the personnel department, told there are no openings, or get screened out by the receptionist. The receptionist wants to know why you are calling.

Speak as if you expect to be connected to the person in charge.

Prepare a response using the following tips:

- Sound businesslike and friendly. Speak as if you *expect* you will get to the right person. Begin by asking for the name of the person in charge of the area where you want to work. Then ask to be connected. In most cases, this will get you through.

- If you have been referred to the person you are calling, say that someone—a friend of the person you are calling—suggested you call.

TIP

Try to get the name of the person in charge before you call. As mentioned in Chapter 6, many companies have Web sites that list contact names and phone numbers. Also, America's Career InfoNet at www.acinet.org gives key contact names and phone numbers for employers in every state.

- If you feel that you are being screened out, say that you want to send some material to the person, and you need the correct spelling of the name, title, and address. (This is true, since you will be sending a resume and JIST Card later.) Then call back tomorrow and ask for the person by name. Or call during lunch, when a replacement receptionist is on the phone.

If you get a voicemail message instead of an operator or receptionist, you can usually reach someone by pressing "O" or holding on the line. When a person answers, follow the previous points. If you get the voicemail of the person in charge, try calling back later.

Situation 2: The supervisor tells you there are no openings at the present time.

Prepare a response using the following tips:

- Don't give up! Show that you are still interested, and again ask for an interview. An employer will often consider a second request.

- Say that although no openings exist at present, you are still very interested and would like to come in anyway to discuss future openings and to talk about the company.

- If you can't get an interview, then ask if it is OK to send a resume and stay in touch. If so, ask if you can call back in about two weeks. Also ask for the names of other organizations that might need someone with your skills.

Situation 3: Because of your good presentation, the employer shows an interest in you and begins to ask you questions over the phone.

Prepare a response using the following tips:

- Ask if you can schedule an interview to cover in person any questions he or she might have. If that doesn't work then...

- Tell him or her more about your special skills, experience, and training that qualify you for the job. Also do the following.

  ✔ Explain why you would be a good employee for this company.

  ✔ Ask questions about the company's service or products. Do *not* ask about pay or benefits.

  ✔ Close with a request for an interview.

Remember: Your main goal is to get an interview.

Contact Employers in Person

You can use your telephone script when making a personal visit to a place of business. Make sure you know your script well and have rehearsed it.

Stopping by a place of business or an organization without an appointment is okay. Some employers will be willing to see you on a short notice.

Goals for Contacting Employers in Person

- Ask to speak to the one person most likely to supervise you. This person also most likely would have the authority to hire you.

- Present your entire telephone script. Do this clearly and without interruption.

- Get an interview! Remember that your goal is to get an interview, so make sure you ask for one.

Ask for an interview...

- For the position you want. *If no, then...*
- To discuss future openings. *If no, then...*
- For information about the organization.

If You Do Not Get an Interview

For employers who can't see you, the visit can still be worthwhile if you do the following:

- Ask to make an appointment for another day and time.

- Leave your JIST Card and resume with the receptionist or supervisor's assistant. Ask that they be passed on to the supervisor.

- Ask for referrals to other companies that may be able to use your skills.

Create Your Final Script

Write out a final script based on your JIST Card. Write it just as you will say it out loud on the phone and in person.

Practice your script and replies by yourself and with others until you feel comfortable and can say your script smoothly.

CHAPTER 8

Contacting Employers in Writing

While phoning and dropping in on potential employers are effective job search methods, you can also try contacting employers in writing. Writing may be your only option for reaching some employers. Examples of when this may happen include the following:

- Ads that require written responses.

- When you are not able to make personal contact with an employer, such as when the employer is rarely available, is on vacation, or is in the office during hours you are at school.

- When the employer tells you to send a cover letter and resume.

- Someone in your network tells you to write to an employer who may be interested in you.

This written communication may be in the following ways:

- By a letter sent through the mail

- By fax

- By e-mail

In most instances, you should include your JIST Card and resume with any correspondence. Resumes are discussed in the next chapter.

What Is a Cover Letter?

Often referred to as a cover letter or letter of application, this correspondence will highlight much of the information you wrote in your telephone script. It should be brief, business-like, and, if possible, addressed to a specific person. A cover letter should accompany your resume.

Source of This Information on Cover Letters

The material and examples on pages 94-102 are based on content from *Creating Your High School Resume: A Step-by-Step Guide to Preparing an Effective Resume for College and Career* by Kathryn Kraemer Troutman. This workbook guides students through the process of creating their first cover letters and resumes. It is published by JIST Works, Inc.

How to Create Great Cover Letters

Without a strong cover letter, your wonderful resume may not get a first glance. The goals of the cover letter are as follows:

- Get potential employers interested in you.

- Impress them with your experience and skills related to a job opening.

- Show your interest in their company and their customers.

- Show that you are dependable, professional, and determined.

- Make employers want to look at your resume.

Let your cover letter highlight your strong points.

The cover letter is as important as your resume. Sample cover letters in this chapter show how to highlight experiences that will interest employers. Do not be bashful about saying that you were a champion swimmer, had a main role in the school play, or are on the school's baseball team. Potential employers will think you are a great student with energy and enthusiasm. They will want you to bring that enthusiasm to their business. Let your cover letter highlight your strong points.

Make Your Cover Letter Look Good

To create a professional look, give your cover letter the same look as your resume. Use the same type fonts and paper stock. Also, do not staple the letter and resume together because employers may want to photocopy your resume easily.

Send the letter and resume in a matching envelope. If you're mailing to a large company, send the resume and letter flat in a large envelope in case your resume will be scanned.

What Is Scanning?

Scanning is a technology that allows resumes to be "read" by Optical Character Readers (OCRs). The resume information is then saved in a computer database and searched by managers looking for employees with certain skills. Scanning is used by large companies to quickly find the most qualified applicants. Scanning is another important reason to use skill-related words in your resume and cover letter. Resumes that will be scanned should be formatted simply—san serif type, no italics, no bullets, and no underlining. This will allow them to be scanned accurately.

Using a job ad from the *Washington Post,* you now will learn how to write a cover letter. We also use other examples here as needed. Here's the *Washington Post* ad:

> **TELEMARKETER.** Enjoys speaking with the public. Articulate, computer literate with sales ability. 40 hours, 12 weeks. Send resume to Mr. Paul Jones, Supervisor, Smythe Corp., 1900 M St., NW, Wash., DC 20006. No calls accepted.

Information About You

Start your cover letter with your contact information. Use the same format and type fonts as on your resume.

Kimberly Ann Garrett
2989 Smithwood Avenue
Annapolis, MD 99999
(555) 555-5555

Date

Next list the date, as you would on any business letter.

May 10, 20XX

Contact Person's Name, Title, Employer, and Address

Then enter the contact person's name, title, employer, and mailing address. You need to have your letter on disk so you can personalize and modify it each time. Because it is so easy to use a computer and save your letter, each letter can be individualized quickly. Here is how to set up the person's name and address:

Mr. Paul Jones
Supervisor
Smythe Corp.
1900 M Street, NW
Washington, DC 20006

But what if you are applying for an advertised job that does not give an individual's name? Then try to find the name of the hiring person or the person reviewing incoming resumes. Put some effort into this research.

> *Using a name can get your letter and resume to the hiring manager more quickly and can be an effective personal touch.*

If you know which department has the opening, you can call the company and ask the operator for the department manager's name. You can also search the company's Web site and try to find the manager's name. If you're applying to a giant corporation and the ad says "Human Resources Director, Marriott Corporation," expect that your resume will be scanned. You may not be able to get an individual's name.

Salutation

Here are your choices for addressing the contact person:

Dear Mr. Jones:	If a man's name is the contact
Dear Ms. Smith:	If a woman's name is the contact
Dear Prospective Employer:	If there is no name or if you're unsure of the person's gender

Opening Paragraph

Here are five types of opening paragraphs, depending on how you learned of the position.

Classified Advertisement

I read your advertisement in the Washington Post *for a Telemarketer on May 10, 20XX.*

Unsolicited Mailing

With an unsolicited mailing, you send companies your resume without being asked or without seeing a specific ad, just in case they need someone like you. Unsolicited resumes are usually not very effective, so try to talk with managers at companies you're interested in before sending resumes.

I would like to apply for a position as Telemarketer with Smythe Corporation. I am seeking a summer position where I can use my communications skills and work with the public.

The Internet

You may find jobs leads on Internet job databases and company Web sites. Here is how to write an opening paragraph for such a lead:

I am sending my attached resume as an application for the Telemarketer position with your company. I found the opening listed on your Web site. Based on the description of Smythe Corporation, I would like to work for a company like yours. I am seeking a position where I can use my communications skills and work with the public.

Referral

A referral is a job lead from a neighbor, friend, mentor, or someone else in your network. Sometimes a person in your network will speak to the hiring person about you. As you learned earlier, this is truly the best way to find a job. Employers appreciate referrals. Referrals save them from reviewing hundreds of applications. Employers trust the recommendation of a valued employee or friend who stated that you would be a good employee. Sometimes departments are filled with the friends of a few people.

Referrals are the greatest!

Here are three sample opening paragraphs for a cover letter based on a referral.

Sample 1. *I am sending my resume to you because of a referral from Mike Thomas, an associate in your Annapolis Store. I am seeking a summer internship where I can use my communications skills and work with the public.*

Sample 2. *I was referred to you by Mike Thomas, who is my neighbor. He tells me that you frequently hire dependable, hard-working high school seniors in your department. Because you spend a great amount of time in the field, Mike recommended that I contact you in writing.*

Sample 3. *I was referred to you by Mike Thomas, who is a member of my church and a longtime family friend. I understand you are hiring student interns in your customer service department. Mike recommended that I write to you and send my resume for your consideration.*

Previous Contact

If an employer you've contacted by phone asks you to send a resume, let your cover letter's opening paragraph remind the employer of your conversation. Don't just send a resume without a cover letter.

I am following up on the conversation we had today by phone. As requested, I am enclosing my resume, which provides more details on my skills and experience.

Middle Paragraph

Next is a summary of your background and critical skills to show you are a match for the position:

As my resume shows, I am active in high school theater and had excellent roles in two plays. I am also successful in debate and student government. With these experiences, I can offer you excellent communication and interpersonal skills. I maintain a 3.0 average and work 10 hours per week during the school year. Familiarity with PCs, Windows, Word, and Excel is another skill I can bring to your department. I use the Internet regularly and can keyboard more than 45 words per minute.

Second Middle Paragraph

This is your persuasive paragraph with a few good-worker traits.

If you are seeking a dependable, hard-working, and friendly young person to work in your department for the summer, I would like to be considered.

Contact Information and Closing

I am available afternoons at (555) 555-5555 after 4 p.m. I have voicemail on that number. I will call you in a couple of days to see if I can make an appointment to discuss a summer position. Thank you for your time and consideration.

Sincerely,

Kimberly Ann Garrett

Kimberly Ann Garrett

Enclosure: resume

If your resume and letter were sent in response to a classified ad with no phone number, or if the company is large and receiving hundreds of resumes, you may not be able to call. In that case, state "I look forward to hearing from you soon."

Think About the Company's Needs

Think about the company's products and services when you write your cover letter. Think about the hiring person's needs. How could you help this person with his or her department? Would you be good with the company's customers? If so, the company would be lucky to have you, right? Get the manager to recognize your interest and talents through your letter and resume.

Cover Letter Samples

The following student is responding to an ad for a part-time position in computer repair. The letter highlights his computer skills and experience. The bullet style is easy to read and write because each entry is a statement, not a full sentence. The paragraph style is written with full sentences. Which one do you prefer?

Here is the ad, followed by the student's letter:

Help Wanted: Computer Technician. Hardware and software experience. Must have Windows conversion experience. Ability to communicate with nontechnical users. One year of experience required. 20 hours/week. Send resume and letter only. Andy E. Quinn, ABC Computers, 322 Smith St., Lockport, NY 20000. No phone calls.

Garth Torres
618 Willingham Road
Little Valley, New York 20000
(555) 555-3333
E-mail: gtorres@com.com

September 18, 20XX

Mr. Andy E. Quinn
ABC Computers
322 Smith Street
Lockport, New York 20000

Dear Mr. Quinn:

I am responding to your advertisement in the *Lockport Gazette* for a Computer Technician in your computer repair business.

Block paragraph style

As a Junior at Little Valley Central High School in Little Valley, New York, I have completed numerous computer courses, including Microsoft Suite and PCs. I have upgraded the hardware and software of my own PC over the last three years. I successfully upgraded my system and friends' PCs to the newest version of Windows. As an assistant in the school's computer lab, I help students with various student computer needs. I am a student support person for the office as well.

Bullet style

I can offer your computer firm the following qualifications:

♦ Junior at Little Valley Central High School, Little Valley, New York, with 20 hours per week available.
♦ Completed five courses in computers, including Microsoft Suite, PC Maintenance, and the Windows Operating System.
♦ Owned and operated PCs for three years.
♦ Installed software, including operating systems and applications programs; upgraded memory and hardware.
♦ Assistant in Computer Lab and school office for eight months; help with 15 PCs.

You will find me to be hard working, energetic, and able to work without supervision. I also communicate well with users and coworkers.

I would like to work part-time throughout my senior year in high school to gain more hands-on experience in computer repair, troubleshooting, and installation. I am available for an interview at your convenience.

Sincerely,

Garth Torres

Garth Torres

Enclosure: Resume

The next letter was sent by a student because of a referral by a teacher, who told him to contact the employer in writing.

Your address and current date

337 North Main Street
Anytown, Pennsylvania 00001
January 10, 20XX

Mr. James Stone
General Manager
Continental Corporation
328 Fifth Avenue
Anytown, Pennsylvania 00001

Name of person and company you are applying to

Dear Mr. Stone:

Mention how you learned of the position

Mention when you are available for employment

I understand from my vocational instructor, Mr. William Jones, that there is now an opening in your department.

As a senior at the County Joint Vocational School in Anytown, Pennsylvania, I will be available for early work placement at the end of January. My previous experience and educational background are outlined in the enclosed resume. I hope you will agree that my background in criminal justice would be an asset to your department. I will be graduating this coming June and expect to receive both my vocational certificate and my high school diploma.

In addition to my experience, I possess skills in organization and communication. I am also reliable and hard working.

May I talk with you about this opening? I will arrange to come for an interview at your convenience. My home telephone number is (555) 555-0000. I look forward to your reply.

Request an interview

Summarize your background and skills to show you are a match for the job

Sincerely,

Jennifer R. York

Sign your name neatly in blue or black ink

Jennifer R. York

Enclosure

Activity

Write a Cover Letter

This worksheet will help you draft a cover letter that can be used in many situations. You can easily modify it to fit the job, employer, and skills needed.

Cover Letter Worksheet

Your street address: _____

Your city, state, zip code: _____

_____

Today's date: _____

Contact person's full name (including Mr. or Ms.): _____

Contact person's title: _____

Contact person's place of employment: _____

Contact person's street address: _____

Contact person's city, state, zip code: _____

_____

Dear Mr./Ms: _____

Opening paragraph. Write a brief statement of why you are sending this letter:

_____

_____

_____

_____

_____

_____

_____

_____

Middle paragraph. Compose a few sentences that would persuade an employer to hire you. Highlight some of your skills and how they would relate to the job.

_____

_____

_____

_____

_____

Second middle paragraph. This is your persuasive paragraph that mentions a few good-worker traits. _____

_____

_____

_____

_____

Final paragraph. Request an interview and include how and when you can be reached. If you know how to reach the employer, mention when you will call as a follow up. _____

_____

_____

_____

_____

Sincerely,

Your signature: _____

Your name typed: _____

Enclosure(s)

Points to Consider When Sending Faxes

An employer may request that you fax your resume. If so, make sure that you include your cover letter so it gets to the right person. It is better, however, to mail the documents or drop them off in person. Your originals will make a stronger impression. You only get one chance to create a first impression, so you want it to be your best.

Another option is to fax your cover letter and resume, and then follow up with copies in the mail.

Points to Consider When Sending E-Mail

Although computers have made it much faster and easier to transmit information, you will lose the quality look of your cover letter and resume by making them part of an e-mail or attaching them to an e-mail. Remember that a first impression may be the only chance you get. Make sure you put your best foot forward.

If an ad or an employer asks you to send your material by e-mail, copy and paste the text into the body of an e-mail rather attaching it as a separate file. An attachment may not be readable if the employer uses different software than you do. You will need to adjust the look of the text in the e-mail so that everything lines up correctly. Then follow up by sending your cover letter and resume in the mail.

Create Your Own Cover Letter

Create a draft copy of your cover letter. Edit and proofread your letter so that it is error free. Check for spelling, grammar, and typographical errors. Don't trust spell checkers alone!

CHAPTER 9

Superior Resumes

You have learned that sending out resumes at random is not an effective job-seeking technique. Many employers, however, will ask you for a resume. They do this because resumes are a useful tool to help them screen people in or out.

A well-done resume will tell an employer who you are and how to contact you. It will give a brief review of your background, work, education, life experience, skills, and abilities in a more detailed manner than the information found on your JIST Card.

The Chronological Resume

While other resume formats exist, most people use a chronological resume. It is a simple resume that presents your experience in reverse chronological order—the most recent experience is listed first, followed by previous experience. As a high school student, you can include sections on your extracurricular activities, achievements, awards, volunteer experiences, and skills.

Look over the following examples of vocational and high school students' resumes and use them as your guide for completing the Resume Worksheet at the end of the chapter.

73990 Smith Valley Road   Phone (555) 999-9999
Medford, California 44444   E-mail shall@netcom.net

Scott Hall

Objective	To attend a four-year college and receive a degree in business.

Education

West Hill High School
Received Diploma June 20XX

1000 Main Street
Medford, California 44444
(555) 999-0000

Awards Received

- **3.8 GPA**
- **Honor Roll (4 years)**
- **Listed in Who's Who Among American High School Students**
- **Americanism and Government Test Winner (2 years)**
- **Northern Conference Scholar Athlete (2 years)**

Work Experience

Summers of 20XX and 20XX

Ken Jones
390 Beloit Road
Medford, California 44444
(555) 555-9999
Loaded/unloaded wagons;
 baled hay

20XX-20XX

City Auto Parts, Inc.
6666 Smith Avenue
Medford, California 44444
(555) 888-4444
Sorted parts; stocked shelves;
 recorded inventory

Volunteer Experience

- Church Youth Group (5 years)
- Northern Canada Missionary Programs (3 years)

Extracurricular Activities

- Future Problem Solving, state champions (4 years)
- Debate (2 years)
- Student Council (2 years)
- Students Against Drunk Driving (3 years)
- Drama, various productions (3 years)

Roberta B. Hired

37 Main Street   **Boise, Idaho 00000**   **(555) 666-7777**   **rhired@connect.com**

OBJECTIVE	To secure a position in the field of Health Technologies or related work.

EDUCATION

September 20XX- June 20XX	Lake County JVS Boise, Idaho	Degree: Vocational Certificate Major: Health Technology Tech Prep
September 20XX- June 20XX	Neighborhood High School Boise, Idaho	Degree: High School Diploma Major: College Prep/Academic

EXPERIENCE

April 20XX- Present	Ashley Place Health Care Boise, Idaho	Position: Nursing Assistant Duties: Provide quality nursing care to residents.
March 20XX- October 20XX	Taco Bell Boise, Idaho	Position: Crew Member Duties: Took and filled customer orders, prepared food items, handled money, and maintained sanitary conditions.
May 20XX- September 20XX	Self-Employed Boise, Idaho	Position: Baby-Sitter Duties: Supervised the safety and activities of children for six families.

ACHIEVEMENTS

Eligible for Emergency Medical Technician (EMT) National Registry Certification
Eligible for American Society of Phlebotomy Technologists (ASPT) Certification
Health Care Provider CPR Certification from the American Heart Association
Honor Roll Student – Freshman through Senior Years
Inducted into the National Honor Society – Junior Year

ACTIVITIES

Vocational Industrial Clubs of America – Two years
Marching Band – Four years
Mentoring experience at Boardman X-Ray

SKILLS

- Medical Terminology
- Anatomy/Physiology
- Computer Literacy
- Phlebotomy
- Emergency Medical Technology

PERSONAL

I take pride in my work, follow directions well, and am willing to learn new skills.
I am dependable, honest, and very hard working. I have an excellent attendance record.

James Cook

5584 Boardman Road   ☐   St. Louis, Missouri 66688   ☐   (333) 555-0000

Objective

To obtain summer employment.

Education

ST. LOUIS HIGH SCHOOL   ST. LOUIS, MISSOURI
Degree: High School Honors Diploma, June 20XX
Major: Academic/College Prep
Rank: Top 15%, 61st of 424 students

National Honor Society, two years
Varsity Football Team, three years, lettered twice
Junior Varsity Football Team, two years
Sophomore Football Team, one year
Freshman Football Team, one year, lettered
Varsity Swim Team, one year, lettered

Volunteer Work

State of Missouri Senior Olympics – set up swim meet; head timer
St. Louis Area Special Olympics – set up swim meet; head timer
St. Louis YMCA – head operator of timing console for home swim meets

Experience

ST. LOUIS COUNTRY CLUB   ST. LOUIS, MISSOURI
Head Golf Caddie   Summers of 20XX and 20XX
Duties included instructing caddies in the proper procedures and
etiquette of golf and caddying for club members.

Awards

Inducted into the National Honor Society
Received two varsity letters in football
Received one varsity letter in swimming
Placed first in the 20XX YCC Pentathlon Swim Meet

Personal

Extremely hard working and dedicated to whatever I am assigned or
attempt to do on my own. Constantly striving to improve and to perform
to the best of my ability.

Krista J. Johnson

317 Wright Avenue	Nashua, New Hampshire 88888
Home Phone (333) 444-4444	Email kjohnson@connect.net

Objective   To obtain a Bachelor of Music Degree in Vocal Performance and Education at a four-year college and also a Master's Degree in Vocal Performance Pedagogy to become a professional singer and voice instructor.

Education   East Fork High School, Nashua, New Hampshire
Graduation expected June 20XX

Work Experience   *September 20XX-current*
Jane's Boutique
2500 West Main Street
Nashua, New Hampshire
(333) 444-8899
Sales Associate

Extracurricular Activities
- Choir (3 years)
- Musicals (leading roles, 3 years)
- Drama (2 years)
- PA Crew (2 years)
- Future Teachers of America (board of directors, 1 year)

Achievements
- Superior Ratings in State Vocal Music Contests (3 years)
- Mount Union College Junior Scholar (2 years)

Volunteer Experience
- Assistant to Vocal Music Teacher (3 years)
- Sang in Area Nursing Homes (2 years)
- Taught Bible School at my church (1 year)

Pat J. Gordon

327 Main Street   Atlanta, Georgia 22222
Home (999) 888-8888   Cell Phone (999) 666-6666

Objective   To secure a position in the field of building, remodeling, and
                    maintenance.

Education

September 20XX-   Local County JVS   Degree: Vocational Certificate
June 20XX   Atlanta, Georgia   Major: Building, Remodeling,
                                            and Maintenance

September 20XX-   Local High School   Degree: High School Diploma
June 20XX   Atlanta, Georgia   Major: College Prep/Business

Experience

April 20XX-   Gates Custom Homes   Position: Carpenter's Assistant
Present   Dunwoody, Georgia   Duties: Lay out cuts, nail
                                            patterns, clean up work area.

March 20XX-   Atlanta Beacon   Position: Paper Carrier
October 20XX   Atlanta, Georgia   Duties: Delivered daily
                                            newspapers to 50 customers;
                                            collected monthly payments;
                                            kept accurate records.

May 20XX-   Self-Employed   Position: Lawn Care
September 20XX   Duties: Mowed and trimmed
                                            yards for six families; pruned
                                            bushes; weeded flower beds.

Achievements   Placed first in regional VICA Carpentry Event, junior year
                    Perfect Attendance Award, senior year
                    Certificate of Achievement in Building and Remodeling

Activities   Vocational Industrial Clubs of America, two years
                    Senior Building, Remodeling, and Maintenance Class
                      President

Skills   Carpentry: framing, decks, roofs, trim, and cabinetry
                    Drywall: hanging, finishing, repairing, and texturing
                    Wiring: residential and EMT
                    Plumbing: basic and residential
                    Siding: vinyl, vertical, and wood
                    Roofing: shingle, gutter, flashing, and drip edge
                    Masonry: brick, block, and pointing
                    Blueprints: draw and read

Professional, Trustworthy, Dependable, Motivated

Describing Your Jobs on Your Resume

Following are commonly held jobs and their required duties. This information may help you complete the Resume Worksheet.

Field	Position	Duties
Fast foods	Crew Member	Take and fill customer orders, operate cash register, and maintain sanitary conditions. (OR) Expedite customer orders at counter and at drive-thru, handle money, and maintain clean and orderly work area.
Baby-sitting	Baby-Sitter for the Robert Smith Family	Supervise the safety and activities of three young children, prepare snacks and meals, and do light housecleaning.
Paper boy	Paper Carrier	Deliver daily newspapers to 50 customers, collect monthly payments, and maintain accurate records.
Medical occupation	Dietary Aid	Prepare trays for residents according to specific dietary needs; sanitize dishes, glassware, utensils, pots, and pans; keep work area clean and orderly.
Child care	Prekindergarten Teacher	Oversee the safety and play of young children and the feeding and changing of infants.

(continues)

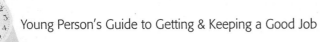
(continued)

Field	Position	Duties
Grocery store	Customer Service	Bag grocery items, assist customers in loading their vehicles, stock and face shelves and displays, maintain clean and orderly conditions.
Grocery store	Cashier	Ring up customer sales using proper store codes; process cash, check, food stamps, and credit card payments; bag items and maintain clean work area.
Lifeguard	Lifeguard	Supervise the safety and activities of patrons; perform CPR and administer first aid when needed; enforce pool rules.
Gas station	Fuel Attendant	Pump gas; wash windows; check fluids; service tires; and process cash, check, and credit card payments.
Landscaping	Landscaper	Seed, sod, mow, weed, fertilize, water, and aerate customer lawns. Plant and transplant shrubs, trees, and flowers. Build rock walls and install fountains.
Lawn care	Lawn Care	Maintain yards for 10 customers; mow, trim, and edge lawns; prune hedges and shrubs; weed and mulch beds.

Field	Position	Duties
Restaurant	Bus Person	Clear, clean, and set tables. Assist servers as needed and maintain sanitary conditions.
Movie theater	Cashier/Usher	Sell and collect movie tickets, expedite snack orders, handle money, stock supplies and food items, direct customers to proper theater areas, and maintain clean conditions.
Fair parking	Parking Attendant	Direct fair traffic to designated parking areas.

Tips for Completing the Resume Worksheet

■ Look up your answers in your *Data Minder.*

■ Complete the Resume Worksheet carefully:

Print neatly in pencil.

Do not abbreviate.

■ Refer to the sample resumes and the section titled "Describing Your Jobs on Your Resume."

Activity

The Resume Worksheet

Use the worksheet that follows to organize your personal information. Review Chapters 3 through 5 for the skills and other details to use in your worksheet. Later, you can use the information from this worksheet to easily create your chronological resume.

Full name: _____

Address: _____

City, state zip code: _____

Area code and phone number: _____

Area code and alternate phone number: _____

E-mail address: _____

Objective   To secure a position in _____

_____

_____

_____

Education

From (month/year)	Name of high school: _____	Degree: _____
To (month/year)	City, state: _____	Major: _____
From (month/year)	Name of high school: _____	Degree: _____
To (month/year)	City, state: _____	Major: _____

Experience   (Most recent job first. Include both paid and unpaid work.)

_____   Company name: _____   Position: _____
From (month/year)

_____   City, state: _____   Duties include: _____
To (month/year)

_____

_____

_____   Company name: _____   Position: _____
From (month/year)

_____   City, state: _____   Duties include: _____
To (month/year)

_____

_____

_____   Company name: _____   Position: _____
From (month/year)

_____   City, state: _____   Duties include: _____
To (month/year)

_____

_____

Achievements   (Include awards, ribbons, trophies, certificates.)

_____

_____

_____

_____

_____

Activities   (Groups, clubs, teams, music. Include number of years of membership or participation.)

_____

_____

_____

(continues)

(continued)

_____

_____

_____

Skills

_____

_____

_____

_____

_____

_____

_____

Personal (Compose three sentences describing your good-worker traits.)

_____

_____

_____

_____

_____

_____

_____

_____

Tips for Preparing a Superior Resume

- **Write it yourself.** It's okay to look at other resumes for ideas, but write yours yourself. It will force you to organize your thoughts and background.

- **Make it error free.** One spelling or grammar error will create a negative impression. Get someone else to review your final draft for errors. Then review it again!

- **Make it look good.** Poor copy quality, cheap paper, bad type quality, or anything that creates a sloppy physical appearance will turn off employers.

- **Be brief and be relevant.** Many good resumes fit on one page. Few justify more than two. Include only the most important points. Use short sentences and action words. If it doesn't relate to and support your job objective, take it out!

- **Be honest.** Don't overstate your qualifications. If you end up getting a job you can't handle, it will not be to your advantage.

- **Be positive.** Emphasize your accomplishments and results. This is no place to be too humble or to display your faults.

- **Be specific.** Rather than saying "I am good with people," say "I supervised four people in the warehouse and increased productivity by 30%." Use numbers whenever possible (people served, percentage increase, dollar increase, and so on).

- **Edit.** Write each of your resume drafts on a separate piece of paper. Make every word count. Keep editing until your resume is as good as you can make it. Then edit it again.

- **Use action words and short sentences.** Look at the sample resumes for ideas.

- **Avoid anything negative.** If an employer might consider anything in your resume as a negative, cut it out.

Tips for Producing Your Resume

- **Review your resume.** Make sure that someone else reviews the final draft. Pick someone who will find spelling, grammar, and other errors. A teacher or counselor is a good choice.

- **Resume formatting.** Use a basic word-processing program to create your resume. Many word-processing programs have resume templates or step-by-step guidance to help you design your resume. If you don't have a home computer, use one at school or the library.

TIP

Be sure to save your resume on a disk for easy updating later.

- **Quality printing.** Output your final resume on a laser printer. Make sure you will be able to produce extra copies as needed.

- **Paper.** Use good-quality paper. If you prefer a color, use ivory, cream, light gray, or any other soft color that can be found in most office-supply stores.

- **Other alternatives.** Take your resume on disk to a local printer and have it printed professionally. Many quick-copy stores provide this service for a small fee.

The Cover Letter

You should always include a cover letter when sending your resume to an employer.

The cover letter should be brief, attract the employer's attention, and introduce you to the employer in a positive and professional way. Use the cover letter you developed in Chapter 8 as a guide. Remember to check the name, title, and address of employers that you are writing to.

CHAPTER 10

Avoiding the Application Trap

Many people think that filling out an application is the same as applying for a job. But it isn't! Most employers use applications to screen people **out**, not in. If your application is messy, incomplete, or shows you do not have the right experience or training, you probably will not get an interview.

Though many smaller employers don't use applications, other employers will ask you to fill out applications. For this reason, it is important to know how to complete them properly.

Activity

Albert C. Smith's Less-Than-Perfect Application

Seeing someone else make mistakes on a job application can help you avoid the same mistakes. Meet Albert C. Smith. Like many of you, he wants to find a job. This activity shows you an application Albert completed at a department store. It is reproduced on the next two pages.

I am sure you will agree that Albert could have done a better job in completing his application. Your job is to review Albert's application and circle the mistakes he made. There are over 30 mistakes in this application. See how many you can find.

Date _April 1_

APPLICATION
FOR EMPLOYMENT

PLEASE PRINT INFORMATION REQUESTED IN INK.

BROWN'S IS AN EQUAL OPPORTUNITY EMPLOYER and fully subscribes to the principles of Equal Employment Opportunity. Brown's has adopted an Affirmative Action Program to ensure that all applicants and employees are considered for hire, promotion and job status, without regard to race, color, religion, sex, national origin, age, handicap, or status as a disabled veteran or veteran of the Vietnam Era.

To protect the interests of all concerned, applicants for certain job assignments must pass a physical examination before they are hired.

Note: This application will be considered active for 90 days. If you have not been employed within this period and are still interested in employment at Brown's, please contact the office where you applied and request that your application be reactivated.

Name _Albert C. Smith_   Social Security Number _411-☰76-2614_
(Please present your Social Security Card for review)

Address _1526 N. Otter_   City   State   Zip Code

County _Marion_   Current phone or nearest phone _____

Previous Address _Same_   Best time of day to contact _any_
(Answer only if position for which you are applying requires driving)

If hired, can you furnish proof of age? ✔ Yes ___ No   Licensed to drive car? ___ Yes ___ No

If hired, can you furnish proof that you are legally entitled to work in U.S. ✔ Yes ___ No   Is license valid in this state? ___ Yes ___ No

Have you ever been employed by Brown's. Yes ___ No _X_ If so, when ___ Position ___

Have you a relative in the employment of Brown's Department Store? Yes ___ No _X_

A PHYSICAL OR MENTAL DISABILITY WILL NOT CAUSE REJECTION IF IN BROWN'S MEDICAL OPINION YOU ARE ABLE TO SATISFACTORILY PERFORM IN THE POSITION FOR WHICH YOU ARE BEING CONSIDERED. Alternative placement, if available, of an applicant who does not meet the physical standards of the job for which he/she was originally considered is permitted.

Do you have any physical or mental impairment which may limit your ability to perform the job for which you are applying? _Yes, I have a back problem & was in Central State Hospital for 6 months._

If yes, what can reasonably be done to accommodate your limitation? _____

	School Attended	No. of Years	Name of School	City/State	Graduate?	Course or College Major	Average Grades
EDUCATION	Grammar	6	Holy Trinity	Scranton	Yes	General	B
	Jr. High	3	Crestview	"	"	"	B
	Sr. High	3	WCHS	"	"	College Prep	C
	Other			"	"		
	College	3	State U	Scranton	NO		C

	Branch of Service	Date Entered Service	Date of Discharge	Highest Rank Held	Service-Related Skills and Experience Applicable to Civilian Employment
MILITARY SERVICE	USA	1995	1998	E-3	☰ radio stuff

What experience or training have you had other than your work experience, military service and education? (Community activities, hobbies, etc.) _____

I am interested in the type of work I have checked:
Sales _X_ Office _X_ Mechanical ☰✔ Warehouse _X_ Other (Specify): ✔
Or the following specific job _anything_

I am seeking (check only one):
✔ Temporary employment (6 days or less)
✔ Seasonal employment (one season, e.g. Christmas)
✔ Regular employment (employment for indefinite period of time)

I am available for (check only one)
✔ Part-Time
✔ Full-Time Work

If part-time, indicate maximum hours per week and enter hours available in block to the right.

If temporary, indicate dates available _____

Have you been convicted during the past seven years of a serious crime involving a person's life or property?
NO _X_ YES ☰ If yes, explain: _drunk in public_

HOURS AVAILABLE FOR WORK	
Sunday	To
Monday	To
Tuesday	To
Wednesday	To _anytime_
Thursday	To
Friday	To
Saturday	To

REFERENCES

LIST BELOW YOUR FOUR MOST RECENT EMPLOYERS, BEGINNING WITH THE CURRENT OR MOST RECENT ONE. IF YOU HAVE HAD FEWER THAN FOUR EMPLOYERS, USE THE REMAINING SPACES FOR PERSONAL REFERENCES. IF YOU WERE EMPLOYED UNDER A MAIDEN OR OTHER NAME, PLEASE ENTER THAT NAME IN THE RIGHT HAND MARGIN. IF APPLICABLE, ENTER SERVICE IN THE ARMED FORCES ON THE REVERSE SIDE.

NAMES AND ADDRESSES OF FORMER EMPLOYERS BEGINNING WITH THE CURRENT OR MOST RECENT	Nature of Employer's Business	Name of Your Supervisor	What kind of work did you do?	Starting Date	Starting Pay	Date of Leaving	Pay at Leaving	Why did you leave? Give details
NOTE: State reason for and length of inactivity between present application date and last employer.								
Name ? Address Walnut St. Tel. No. City Scranton State Zip Code	School	Eric Burgess	Clean up	Month ? 99 Year	$7 an hr Per Week	Month Present		Fired
NOTE: State reason for and length of inactivity between present application date and last employer.								
Name Fred Willis Tel. No. ? Address City Scranton State PA Zip Code	Houses	Rafael	electrical helper — laborer	Month 7 98 Year	$6.50 an hr Per Week	Month looked for a job — almost a year	$6.50 Per Week	Boss always picked on me.
NOTE: State reason for and length of inactivity between present application date and last employer.								
Name Wayne Condor Tel. No. Address 1436 N. Anderson 555-4141 City Scranton State PA Zip Code	Construction	Jack Kimberski	jack hammer + wiring	Month 6 93 Year	$6 an hr Per Week	Month 4 94 Year	$6.25 Per Week	Company went broke.
NOTE: State reason for and length of inactivity between present application date and last employer.								
Name Central Hospital Tel. No. Address Washington St. City Scranton State PA Zip Code	Mental Hospital	Lynn Donovan	Clean up	Month ? Year	$5.50 an hr Per Week	Month ? Year	same	I got better + was discharged.

I certify that the information in this application is correct to the best of my knowledge and understand that any misstatement or omission of information is grounds for dismissal in accordance with Brown's policy. I authorize the references listed above to give you any and all information concerning my previous employment and any pertinent information they may have, personal or otherwise, and release all parties from all liability for any damage that may result from furnishing same to you. In consideration of my employment, I agree to conform to the rules and regulations of Brown's, and my employment and compensation can be terminated with or without cause, and with or without notice, at any time, at the option of either the Company or myself. I understand that no unit manager or representative of Brown's other than the President or Vice-President of the company, has any authority to enter into any agreement for employment for any specified period of time, or to make any agreement contrary to the foregoing. In some states, the law requires that Brown's have my written permission before obtaining consumer reports on me, and I hereby authorize Brown's to obtain such reports.

Applicant's Signature _Smith, Albert C._

NOT TO BE FILLED OUT BY APPLICANT

			(Store will enter dates as required.)	Mailed	Completed
Date of Emp.		REFERENCE REQUESTS		not yet	
Dept or Div.	Regular ___ Part-time ___	Physical examination scheduled for ~~didn't~~	CONSUMER REPORT		
Job Title	Job Grade	Physical examination form completed I didn't get one.	With Tax (W-4)		
Job Title Code			State With Tax		
Compensation Arrangement Make me an offer		Review Card prepared	Minor's Work Permit		
Manager Approving		Timecard prepared	Proof of Birth		
Employee No.			Training Material Given to Employee		

INTERVIEWER'S COMMENTS: _I really need a job now._

Prospect for 1. 2.

Rack No. ___

Unit Name and Number _Albert Smith_

Activity

Albert C. Smith's Improved Application

Albert C. Smith's application has many mistakes. How many did you find? It would not make a good impression on any employer. It is messy, includes negative information, and has many other problems.

The example on pages 126-127 shows what Albert C. Smith's application looked like when properly filled out.

Look it over and see how many errors you found that were corrected on the improved version.

A messy job application does not make a good impression.

You can make only one first impression, so let it be positive.

Remember that applications are designed to screen you out of a job.

Young Person's Guide to Getting & Keeping a Good Job

Date **April 1, 2000**

APPLICATION FOR EMPLOYMENT

BROWN'S IS AN EQUAL OPPORTUNITY EMPLOYER and fully subscribes to the principles of Equal Employment Opportunity. Brown's has adopted an Affirmative Action Program to ensure that all applicants and employees are considered for hire, promotion and job status, without regard to race, color, religion, sex, national origin, age, handicap, or status as a disabled veteran or veteran of the Vietnam Era.

To protect the interests of all concerned, applicants for certain job assignments must pass a physical examination before they are hired.

PLEASE PRINT INFORMATION REQUESTED IN INK.

Note: This application will be considered active for 90 days. If you have not been employed within this period and are still interested in employment at Brown's, please contact the office where you applied and request that your application be reactivated.

Name **Smith** **Albert** **Claude**
     Last   First   Middle

Social Security Number **411-76-2614**
(Please present your Social Security Card for review)

Address **1526** **North Otter Street** **Scranton** **PA** **18602**
       Number   Street   City   State   Zip Code

County _____

Previous Address _____
               Number   Street   City   State   Zip Code

Current phone or nearest phone **555-1212**

Best time of day to contact **after 12 p.m.**

(Answer only if position for which you are applying requires driving)

If hired, can you furnish proof of age? **✓** Yes ____ No

Licensed to drive car? **✓** Yes ____ No

If hired, can you furnish proof that you are legally entitled to work in U.S. **✓** Yes ____ No

Is license valid in this state? **✓** Yes ____ No

Have you ever been employed by Brown's?   Yes ____   No **✓**   If so, when ____   Position ____

Have you a relative in the employment of Brown's Department Store?   Yes ____   No **✓**

A PHYSICAL OR MENTAL DISABILITY WILL NOT CAUSE REJECTION IF IN BROWN'S MEDICAL OPINION YOU ARE ABLE TO SATISFACTORILY PERFORM IN THE POSITION FOR WHICH YOU ARE BEING CONSIDERED. Alternative placement, if available, of an applicant who does not meet the physical standards of the job for which he/she was originally considered is permitted.

Do you have any physical or mental impairment which may limit your ability to perform the job for which you are applying? **No**

If yes, what can reasonably be done to accommodate your limitation? _____

	School Attended	No. of Years	Name of School	City/State	Graduate?	Course or College Major	Average Grades
EDUCATION	Grammar	6	Holy Trinity	Scranton, PA		General	B
	Jr. High	3	Crestview Junior H.S.	Scranton, PA		General	B
	Sr. High	3	Warren Central H.S.	Scranton, PA	—	College Prep	C
	Other	—			—		
	College	3	Indiana-Purdue University at Indpls	Indpls, IN		Electronics in progress	B

	Branch of Service	Date Entered Service	Date of Discharge	Highest Rank Held	Service-Related Skills and Experience Applicable to Civilian Employment
MILITARY SERVICE	United States Air Force	6-2-94	4-15-98	A/1C Airman First Class	Radio and small electronics repair

What experience or training have you had other than your work experience, military service and education? (Community activities, hobbies, etc.) _____

I am interested in the type of work I have checked:

Sales **✓**   Office ____   Mechanical ____   Warehouse ____   Other (Specify): **Repair**

Or the following specific job _____

I am seeking (check only one):

____ Temporary employment (6 days or less)

____ Seasonal employment (one season, e.g. Christmas)

✓ Regular employment (employment for indefinite period of time)

I am available for (check only one):

____ Part-Time

✓ Full-Time

____ If part-time, indicate maximum hours per week and enter hours available in block to the right.

If temporary, indicate dates available _____

Have you been convicted during the past seven years of a serious crime involving a person's life or property?

NO **✓**   YES ____   If yes, explain: _____

HOURS AVAILABLE FOR WORK		
Sunday	8 a.m.	To close
Monday	8 a.m.	To close
Tuesday	8 a.m.	To close
Wednesday	8 a.m.	To close
Thursday	8 a.m.	To close
Friday	8 a.m.	To close
Saturday	8 a.m.	To close

© JIST Works, Inc., Indianapolis, IN

REFERENCES

LIST BELOW YOUR FOUR MOST RECENT EMPLOYERS, BEGINNING WITH THE CURRENT OR MOST RECENT ONE. IF YOU HAVE HAD FEWER THAN FOUR EMPLOYERS, USE THE REMAINING SPACES FOR PERSONAL REFERENCES. IF YOU WERE EMPLOYED UNDER A MAIDEN OR OTHER NAME, PLEASE ENTER THAT NAME IN THE RIGHT HAND MARGIN. IF APPLICABLE, ENTER SERVICE IN THE ARMED FORCES ON THE REVERSE SIDE.

NAMES AND ADDRESSES OF FORMER EMPLOYERS BEGINNING WITH THE CURRENT OR MOST RECENT	Nature of Employer's Business	Name of Your Supervisor	What kind of work did you do?	Starting Date	Starting Pay	Date of Leaving	Pay at Leaving	Why did you leave? Give details
Name Fred Willis / Address 1275 E. 17th St. Tel. No. 555-2111 / City Scranton State PA Zip Code 18515	Electrical sub-contractor	Rafael Castillo	Electrician helper	Month 8 / Year 99	$280 Per Week	Month Present / Year	$280 Per Week	Work slowdown — limited work schedule
NOTE: State reason for and length of inactivity between present application date and last employer. Did odd/independent jobs, college courses — 5 months								
Name Scranton Public Schools / Address 593 Walnut Ave. Tel. No. 555-3111 / City Scranton State PA Zip Code 18505	Maintenance of school	Eric Burgess	Custodian	Month 7 / Year 98	$260 Per Week	Month 3 / Year 99	$260 Per Week	Desired a more demanding position
NOTE: State reason for and length of inactivity between present application date and last employer.								
Name Grand Forks Air Force Base - USAF / Address Hwy 2 Tel. No. 701-597-2112 / City Grand Forks State ND Zip Code 58211	U.S. Air Force	Technical Sergeant Denise Hager	Small electronics + radio repair	Month 1 / Year 95	$250 Per Week	Month 4 / Year 98	$275 Per Week	Term of service expired — Honorable Discharge
NOTE: State reason for and length of inactivity between present application date and last employer. Completed basic training + electronics repair school — 6 mos.								
Name Wayne Construction / Address 1436 N. Anderson Dr. Tel. No. 555-4141 / City Scranton State PA Zip Code 18509	Heavy + light constr.	Kim Lenski	Electronic equipment installer	Month 6 / Year 93	$240 Per Week	Month 4 / Year 94	$250 Per Week	Company went out of business — joined U.S. Air Force

Applicant's Signature ___Albert C. Smith___

NOT TO BE FILLED OUT BY APPLICANT

(Store will enter dates as required)

	Mailed	Completed
REFERENCE REQUESTS		
CONSUMER REPORT		
With Tax (W-4)		
State With Tax		

Tested	
Physical examination scheduled for	
Physical examination form completed	

Review Card prepared		Minor's Work Permit	
Timecard prepared		Proof of Birth	
		Training Material Given to Employee	

INTERVIEWER'S COMMENTS

Date of Emp.	
Dept. or Div.	Regular ___ / Part-time ___
Job Title	
Job Title Code	Job Grade
Compensation Arrangement	
Manager Approving	
Employee No.	Rack No.

Prospect for
1.
2.

Unit Name and Number _____

Activity

Complete a Sample Job Application

Now you are ready to complete an application yourself. In completing your own application, be as neat and as thorough as possible. You have already gathered much of the information you need in earlier chapters and in your *Data Minder*. Refer to them as needed.

An application may not get you a job, but it can get you screened out of being interviewed for one. Look over the completed application that follows. It will give you an idea of how to complete one. Then, complete the blank application and remember to do the following:

- Use your *Data Minder* to find the details needed on your application.

- Follow instructions. Read everything carefully before completing each section.

- Use an erasable black pen.

- Be neat. Take your time and avoid crossouts.

- Be accurate. Do not guess at an answer.

- Fill in every blank. Use "NA" (does not apply) or a short dash when something does not apply to you.

- Be honest. Being dishonest could lead to dismissal from a job. But don't include negative information.

- Write clearly and neatly. You can make only one impression, so make it a good one.

- Emphasize your skills and accomplishments. Find a place to mention your strengths even if the application does not ask for them.

- If you are short on paid work experience, mention your volunteer work and related hobbies under the former employers' section.

- Get permission before using a reference.

- Sign the application if requested.

Remember to act as if you were completing this application to get the job that you really want. Good luck!

More Hints on Completing Applications

■ Dress appropriately when you pick up, fill out, or drop off applications from employers.

■ Do not bring anyone with you when applying for jobs or going on interviews.

■ If possible, complete applications at home so you can fill them out with the greatest care.

■ Be sure to proofread your applications to correct any errors.

■ Try to meet employers to hand in applications directly and ask for interviews. If unable to do so, be sure to call each employer after a few days to make sure the employer received your application. Tell the employer that you are still interested in the position and then set up an interview. Remember: You can make only one first impression, so let it be positive.

Be prepared and have time for an interview—just in case.

APPLICATION FOR EMPLOYMENT

(Pre-Employment Questionnaire)   (An Equal Opportunity Employer)

A. PERSONAL INFORMATION

DATE 11-6-XX

SOCIAL SECURITY NUMBER 000-00-0000

NAME Hired (LAST) Robert (FIRST) Brian (MIDDLE)

PRESENT ADDRESS 37 Main Street (STREET) Anytown (CITY) Utah (STATE) 55555 (ZIP)

PERMANENT ADDRESS 37 Main Street (STREET) Anytown (CITY) Utah (STATE) 55555 (ZIP)

PHONE NO. (555) 555-0000   ARE YOU 18 YEARS OR OLDER? ☒ YES ☐ NO

ARE YOU EITHER A U.S. CITIZEN OR AN ALIEN AUTHORIZED TO WORK IN THE UNITED STATES? ☒ YES ☐ NO

B. EMPLOYMENT DESIRED

POSITION Security   DATE YOU CAN START immediately SALARY DESIRED open

ARE YOU EMPLOYED NOW? yes   IF SO, MAY WE INQUIRE OF YOUR PRESENT EMPLOYER? yes

EVER APPLIED TO THIS COMPANY BEFORE? no WHERE? ——— WHEN? ———

REFERRED BY Mr. George Ward

C. EDUCATION	NAME AND LOCATION OF SCHOOL	NO. OF YEARS ATTENDED	DID YOU GRADUATE?	SUBJECTS STUDIED
GRAMMAR SCHOOL	Main Street Elem. Anytown, UT / Town Center Middle School Anytown, UT	9 yrs. (gr. K-8th)	yes	general
HIGH SCHOOL	Center High School Anytown, UT	2 yrs. (gr. 9th-10th)	will graduate 6/xx	general
COLLEGE	n/a	—	—	—
TRADE, BUSINESS, OR CORRESPONDENCE SCHOOL	County J.V.S. Anytown, UT	2 yrs. (gr. 11th-12th)	will graduate 6/xx	Criminal Justice

D. GENERAL

SUBJECTS OF SPECIAL STUDY OR RESEARCH WORK Senior in a two-year vocational Criminal Justice program. Receiving over 1500 hours of hands-on training.

SPECIAL SKILLS Certified in CPR. Trained in patrolling, dispatching, radio ✱

ACTIVITIES (CIVIC, ATHLETIC, ETC.) Vocational Industrial Clubs of America (2 years)

EXCLUDE ORGANIZATIONS, THE NAME OF WHICH INDICATES THE RACE, CREED, SEX, AGE, MARITAL STATUS, COLOR, OR NATION OF ORIGIN OF ITS MEMBERS.

U.S. MILITARY OR NAVAL SERVICE n/a RANK —   PRESENT MEMBERSHIP IN NATIONAL GUARD OR RESERVES —

✱ communications, arrest procedures, self-defense, and computer operations.

E. FORMER EMPLOYERS. LIST BELOW LAST FOUR EMPLOYERS, STARTING WITH LAST ONE FIRST.

DATE MONTH AND YEAR	NAME AND ADDRESS OF EMPLOYER	SALARY	POSITION	REASON FOR LEAVING
FROM 6-XX TO present	IGA 300 West St., Nearby, UT	$5^{15}	Customer service	n/a
FROM 11-XX TO 6-XX	McDonald's 1005 East St., Local, UT	$4^{75}	crew member	scheduling
FROM 5-XX TO 9-XX	The Smith Family 919 Park St., Local, UT	$15^{00}	lawn care	seasonal
FROM TO				

F. REFERENCES. GIVE THE NAMES OF THREE PERSONS NOT RELATED TO YOU, WHOM YOU HAVE KNOWN AT LEAST ONE YEAR.

NAME	PHONE NUMBER	BUSINESS	YEARS ACQUAINTED
1. Mr. George Ward	(555) 555-2222	Vocational Instructor at County J.V.S.	2
2. Mr. John Rocklin	(555) 555-3333	Retired GM Worker	3
3. Mrs. Susan Hughes	(555) 555-4444	Manager at McDonald's	1 ½

G. PHYSICAL RECORD

DO YOU HAVE ANY PHYSICAL LIMITATIONS THAT PRECLUDE YOU FROM PERFORMING ANY WORK FOR WHICH YOU ARE BEING CONSIDERED? ☐ YES ☒ NO   IF YES, WHAT CAN BE DONE TO ACCOMMODATE YOUR LIMITATION?

n/a

IN CASE OF EMERGENCY, NOTIFY Grace Hired 37 Main Street Anytown, UT 55555 (555) 555-0000
NAME (mother) ADDRESS PHONE NO.

"I CERTIFY THAT THE FACTS CONTAINED IN THIS APPLICATION ARE TRUE AND COMPLETE TO THE BEST OF MY KNOWLEDGE AND UNDERSTAND THAT, IF EMPLOYED, FALSIFIED STATEMENTS ON THIS APPLICATION SHALL BE GROUNDS FOR DISMISSAL.

I AUTHORIZE INVESTIGATION OF ALL STATEMENTS CONTAINED HEREIN AND THE REFERENCES LISTED ABOVE TO GIVE YOU ANY AND ALL INFORMATION CONCERNING MY PREVIOUS EMPLOYMENT AND ANY PERTINENT INFORMATION THEY MAY HAVE, PERSONAL OR OTHERWISE, AND RELEASE ALL PARTIES FROM ALL LIABILITY FOR ANY DAMAGE THAT MAY RESULT FROM FURNISHING SAME TO YOU.

I UNDERSTAND AND AGREE THAT, IF HIRED, MY EMPLOYMENT IS FOR NO DEFINITE PERIOD AND MAY, REGARDLESS OF THE DATE OF PAYMENT OF MY WAGES AND SALARY, BE TERMINATED AT ANY TIME WITHOUT ANY PRIOR NOTICE."

DATE 11-6-XX   SIGNATURE Robert B. Hired

DO NOT WRITE BELOW THIS LINE

INTERVIEWED BY _____   DATE _____

_____

_____

_____

HIRED ☐ YES ☐ NO   POSITION _____   DEPT. _____

SALARY/WAGE _____   DATE REPORTING TO WORK _____

APPROVED: 1. _____ 2. _____ 3. _____
EMPLOYMENT MANAGER DEPT. HEAD GENERAL MANAGER

APPLICATION FOR EMPLOYMENT
(Pre-Employment Questionnaire)   (An Equal Opportunity Employer)

A. PERSONAL INFORMATION

DATE _____

SOCIAL SECURITY
NUMBER _____

NAME _____

LAST   FIRST   MIDDLE

PRESENT ADDRESS _____

STREET   CITY   STATE   ZIP

PERMANENT ADDRESS _____

STREET   CITY   STATE   ZIP

PHONE NO. _____ ARE YOU 18 YEARS OR OLDER? ❏ YES ❏ NO

ARE YOU EITHER A U.S. CITIZEN OR AN ALIEN AUTHORIZED TO WORK IN THE UNITED STATES? ❏ YES ❏ NO

B. EMPLOYMENT DESIRED

POSITION _____ DATE YOU CAN START _____ SALARY DESIRED _____

ARE YOU EMPLOYED NOW? _____ IF SO, MAY WE INQUIRE OF YOUR PRESENT EMPLOYER? _____

EVER APPLIED TO THIS COMPANY BEFORE? _____ WHERE? _____ WHEN? _____

REFERRED BY _____

C. EDUCATION	NAME AND LOCATION OF SCHOOL	NO. OF YEARS ATTENDED	DID YOU GRADUATE?	SUBJECTS STUDIED
GRAMMAR SCHOOL				
HIGH SCHOOL				
COLLEGE				
TRADE, BUSINESS, OR CORRESPONDENCE SCHOOL				

D. GENERAL

SUBJECTS OF SPECIAL STUDY OR RESEARCH WORK _____

_____

SPECIAL SKILLS _____

ACTIVITIES (CIVIC, ATHLETIC, ETC.) _____

EXCLUDE ORGANIZATIONS, THE NAME OF WHICH INDICATES THE RACE, CREED, SEX, AGE, MARITAL STATUS, COLOR, OR NATION OF ORIGIN OF ITS MEMBERS.

U.S. MILITARY OR

NAVAL SERVICE _____ RANK _____

PRESENT MEMBERSHIP IN NATIONAL

GUARD OR RESERVES _____

E. FORMER EMPLOYERS. LIST BELOW LAST FOUR EMPLOYERS, STARTING WITH LAST ONE FIRST.

DATE MONTH AND YEAR	NAME AND ADDRESS OF EMPLOYER	SALARY	POSITION	REASON FOR LEAVING
FROM				
TO				
FROM				
TO				
FROM				
TO				
FROM				
TO				

F. REFERENCES. GIVE THE NAMES OF THREE PERSONS NOT RELATED TO YOU, WHOM YOU HAVE KNOWN AT LEAST ONE YEAR.

NAME	PHONE NUMBER	BUSINESS	YEARS ACQUAINTED
1.			
2.			
3.			

G. PHYSICAL RECORD

DO YOU HAVE ANY PHYSICAL LIMITATIONS THAT PRECLUDE YOU FROM PERFORMING ANY WORK FOR WHICH YOU ARE BEING CONSIDERED? ☐ YES ☐ NO   IF YES, WHAT CAN BE DONE TO ACCOMMODATE YOUR LIMITATION?

_____

_____

IN CASE OF EMERGENCY, NOTIFY _____
                                      NAME   ADDRESS   PHONE NO.

"I CERTIFY THAT THE FACTS CONTAINED IN THIS APPLICATION ARE TRUE AND COMPLETE TO THE BEST OF MY KNOWLEDGE AND UNDERSTAND THAT, IF EMPLOYED, FALSIFIED STATEMENTS ON THIS APPLICATION SHALL BE GROUNDS FOR DISMISSAL.

I AUTHORIZE INVESTIGATION OF ALL STATEMENTS CONTAINED HEREIN AND THE REFERENCES LISTED ABOVE TO GIVE YOU ANY AND ALL INFORMATION CONCERNING MY PREVIOUS EMPLOYMENT AND ANY PERTINENT INFORMATION THEY MAY HAVE, PERSONAL OR OTHERWISE, AND RELEASE ALL PARTIES FROM ALL LIABILITY FOR ANY DAMAGE THAT MAY RESULT FROM FURNISHING SAME TO YOU.

I UNDERSTAND AND AGREE THAT, IF HIRED, MY EMPLOYMENT IS FOR NO DEFINITE PERIOD AND MAY, REGARDLESS OF THE DATE OF PAYMENT OF MY WAGES AND SALARY, BE TERMINATED AT ANY TIME WITHOUT ANY PRIOR NOTICE."

DATE _____ SIGNATURE _____

DO NOT WRITE BELOW THIS LINE

INTERVIEWED BY _____ DATE _____

_____

_____

HIRED ☐ YES ☐ NO POSITION _____ DEPT. _____

SALARY/WAGE _____ DATE REPORTING TO WORK _____

APPROVED: 1. _____ 2. _____ 3. _____
                EMPLOYMENT MANAGER   DEPT. HEAD   GENERAL MANAGER

CHAPTER 11

The Interview

Very few people get a job without an interview. It is a very important part of the job search process. The interview provides employers with the chance to get to know you. It provides you with the same opportunity—a chance to get to know them.

The Interview and Employer's Expectations

Employers use an interview to evaluate you. Will you be able to do the job? Will you be a good employee? If employers don't believe you are qualified and willing to work hard, you won't get a job offer. But if you do well in the interview, you are much more likely to get a job offer—or a referral. So you need to know what to do and say in a job interview.

You looked at employer expectations in Chapter 2. Because they are so important, let's review them again here.

Expectation 1: Appearance (or, Do You Look Like the Right Person?)

Remember that employers will react to first impressions. So how you come across in the first few minutes is very important.

> *If you do well in the interview, you are more likely to get a job offer.*

- **Personal appearance.** If you do not look like the right person or if your appearance is "wrong," an employer will be turned off immediately.

- **Manner.** Arrive early and be relaxed. Be polite with the receptionist or other staff. Greet the employer in a friendly way, and shake hands if offered. During the interview, be aware of how you look to the interviewer. For example, leaning forward a bit in your chair helps you look interested and alert. Smiling and looking at the interviewer as he or she speaks helps you seem more confident.

- **Paperwork.** Your application, JIST Card, resume, and portfolio create an impression. Are they neat, error free, accurate, and filled out completely?

- **Communications.** Speak in a distinct, clear voice. Use proper grammar. Emphasize the things you can do well and a willingness to try hard. Be honest and open with your answers.

Expectation 2: Attendance, Punctuality, Reliability (or, Can You Be Counted On?)

Remember that all employers want someone they can depend on. Keep these points in mind:

- **Daily attendance and punctuality.** Be early for the interview. Mention your good attendance record at school or other jobs.

- **Dependability.** Employers want to hire people they can trust to do the job. Many questions that employers ask during interviews will give you a chance to show that you are reliable. It is very important that you tell them.

Expectation 3: Skills, Experience, Training (or, Can You Do the Job?)

Emphasize what you can do. Think in advance what the job requires and emphasize points that support your doing it well.

Be sure to emphasize your skills.

- **Skills.** Employers will want to know your skills. Review your skills lists from Chapter 3 to remind yourself what you can do. Because you will probably compete with job seekers who have more work experience, emphasize your self-management and transferable skills in your interview responses.

Other points to discuss include the following:

- **Experience**
- **Education and training**
- **Interests and hobbies**
- **Life experience**
- **Achievements**

Remember: Employers Are Evaluating You

In one way or another, interviewers must find out about all the preceding issues. At every point in the interview process, they are evaluating you—even when you might least expect it.

The following section breaks the interview into six phases. As you learn to handle each one, you will be better able to meet an employer's expectations. Then you will be much more likely to get a job offer.

Six Phases of an Interview

No two interviews are alike. But there are similarities. If you look closely at the interview process, you can see separate phases. Looking at each phase will help you learn how to handle interviews well. The phases are as follows:

1. Before the interview

2. Opening moves

3. The interview itself

4. Closing the interview

5. Following up

6. Making a final decision

Every step of the interview is important. The following sections show you why and give you tips for handling each phase.

✔ Phase 1: Before the Interview

An interviewer can make judgments about you in many ways before you meet. For example, you may have spoken to the interviewer or the interviewer's assistant on the phone. You may have sent the interviewer a resume or other correspondence. Or someone may have told the interviewer about you.

Be careful in all your early contacts with an employer. Do everything possible to create a good impression.

Before you meet an interviewer, here are some things to consider:

Dress and Grooming

How you dress and groom for an interview varies from job to job. You will have to make your own decisions about what is right for each interview situation. Because there are so many differences, there are no firm rules on how to dress. But you should avoid certain things. Here are some important tips:

- **Don't wear jeans, tank tops, shorts, or other very casual clothes.**

- **Be conservative.** An interview is not a good time to be trendy.

- **Check your shoes.** Little things count, so pay attention to everything you wear.

- **Be conservative with cologne, aftershave, makeup, and jewelry.**

- **Careful grooming is a must.** Get those hands and nails extra clean and manicured. Eliminate stray facial hairs.

- **Spend some money if necessary.** Get one well-fitting interview outfit.

Do Some Research

Know as much as you can about the organization before you go to an important interview. Find out about the following:

- **The organization**
  - ✔ Major products or services
  - ✔ Number of employees
  - ✔ Reputation
  - ✔ Values

- **The position**
  - ✔ Does an opening exist?
  - ✔ Salary range and benefits
  - ✔ Duties and responsibilities

Get There Early

Get to the interview a few minutes early. Make sure you know how to get there, and allow plenty of time. Call for directions if necessary.

Final Grooming

Before you go in for the interview, stop in a rest room. Look at yourself in a mirror and make any final adjustments.

Waiting Room Behavior

Assume that interviewers will hear about everything you do in the waiting room. They will ask the receptionist how you conducted yourself—and how you treated the receptionist.

The Receptionist

The receptionist's opinion of you matters. So go out of your way to be polite and friendly. If you spoke to the receptionist on the phone, mention that and express appreciation for any help you were offered.

If the Interviewer Is Late

If the interviewer is late, you are lucky. The interviewer will probably feel bad about keeping you waiting and may give you better-than-average treatment to make up for it.

If you have to wait over 20 minutes or so, ask to reschedule your appointment. You don't want to act as if you have nothing to do. And, again, the interviewer may make it up to you later.

✔ Phase 2: Opening Moves

The first few minutes of an interview are very important. If you make a bad impression, you probably won't be able to change it. Interviewers react to many things you say and do during the first few minutes of an interview. Here are some points they mention most often:

Initial Greeting

Be ready for a friendly greeting. Show you are happy to be there. Although this is a business meeting, your social skills will be considered. A firm—but not crushing—handshake is needed unless the interviewer does not offer to shake hands.

Posture

How you stand and sit can make a difference. You look more interested if you lean forward in your chair when talking or listening. If you lean back, you may look *too* relaxed.

Voice

You may be nervous, but try to sound enthusiastic. Your voice should be neither too soft nor too loud.

TIP

Practice sounding confident. It will help you feel confident.

Eye Contact

People who don't look in the speaker's eyes are considered shy, insecure, and even dishonest. Although you should never stare, you seem more confident when you look in the interviewer's eyes while you listen or speak.

Distracting Habits

You may have nervous habits you don't even notice. But pay attention! Most interviewers find such habits annoying. For example, do you play with your hair or say something like "you know" over and over? (You know what I mean?)

The best way to see yourself as others do is to have someone videotape you while you role-play an interview. If that is not possible, become aware of how others see you and try to change negative behavior.

TIP

Your friends and relatives can help you notice any annoying habits you have that could bother an interviewer.

Establishing the Relationship

Almost all interviews begin with informal small talk. Favorite subjects are the weather and whether you had trouble getting there. This chatting seems to have nothing to do with the interview. But it does. These first few minutes allow an interviewer to relax you and find out how you relate to each other.

You can do many things during the first few minutes of an interview. The following are some suggestions from experienced interviewers:

- **Allow things to happen.** Relax. Don't feel you have to start a serious interview right away.

- **Smile.** Look happy to be there and to meet the interviewer.

- **Use the interviewer's name.** Be formal. Use "Mr. Stewart" or "Ms. Evans" unless you are asked to use another name. Use the interviewer's name as often as you can in your conversation.

✓ Phase 3: The Interview Itself

This is the most complex part of the interview. It can last from 15 to 45 minutes or more while the interviewer tries to find your strengths and weaknesses.

Interviewers may ask you almost anything. They are looking for any problems you may have. They also want to be convinced that you have the skills, experience, and personality to do a good job. If you have made a good impression so far, you can use this phase to talk about your qualifications.

You will learn how to create a career portfolio in Chapter 12. Take it with you to the interview and present it to the employer. Be sure to point out the most relevant and impressive elements in your portfolio. Leave copies of these items with the employer.

How to Answer Problem Questions

In one survey, employers said that over 90 percent of the people they interviewed could not answer problem questions. Over 80 percent could not explain the skills they had for the job. This is a serious problem for most job seekers. It keeps many of them from getting a good job that will use their skills.

There are hundreds of questions an interviewer might ask you in an interview. It would be impossible for you to have answers prepared for all of them. A better approach is to learn a technique to answering most interview questions.

Interviewers may ask you almost anything.

© JIST Works, Inc., Indianapolis, IN

Three Steps to Answering Problem Questions

1. **Understand what is really being asked.**

   Most employers are trying to find out about your self-management skills. While rarely this blunt, the employer's real questions are often the following:

   - Can I depend on you?
   - Are you easy to get along with?
   - Are you a good worker?

   The question may also be the following:

   - Do you have the experience and training to do the job if I hire you?

2. **Answer the question briefly.**

   - Acknowledge the facts, but...
   - Present them as an advantage, not a disadvantage.

3. **Answer the real concern by presenting your related skills.**

   - Base your answer on your key skills from your lists in Chapter 3.
   - Give examples to support your skills statements.

Activity

Answer Problem Questions

This activity will help you form answers to the most common problem interview questions. Here are a few pointers:

- Write out complete and honest answers for each question.
- Suggestions are included to help you prepare answers that will stand out and impress employers. Don't forget to give lots of examples.
- A good answer should take between 30 seconds and two minutes.
- Sell yourself!

Problem Questions Worksheet

1. Can you tell me a little about yourself?

Suggestions

Talk about your education: when you're graduating, what you're majoring in, and what your achievements are.

Talk about your experience in both related and unrelated jobs.

Talk about your good-worker traits.

2. Why are you applying for this type of job and why here? _____

Suggestions

You discovered through training that you enjoy and are good at this type of work.

You noticed the company's ad; got a referral from someone; know the company has an excellent reputation; and so on.

3. What training or experience qualifies you for this position? _____

Suggestion
Refer to Chapter 4 and your *Data Minder* pages 4-15 and 21.

_____

_____

_____

_____

_____

4. What are the greatest strengths you would bring to this job? _____

Suggestions
Refer to Chapter 3 and *Data Minder* pages 7 and 21 for your job-related, self-management, and transferable skills.

Talk about your best skills and use examples to prove them.

_____

_____

_____

_____

_____

5. What do you consider your greatest weakness? _____

Suggestions
Never say that you don't have any weaknesses or that you cannot think of any.

Never talk about a weakness that will prevent you from being hired.

Mention a job skill you have not learned yet or have trouble doing well.

Say something positive after you mention a weakness, such as "But I'm anxious to learn" or "But I can do such-and-such well."

Say that you tend to ask lots of questions when starting a job, but it's because you want to do your work correctly.

_____

_____

_____

_____

_____

(continues)

(continued)

6. How much do you expect to be paid? _____

_____

Suggestions

Research pay rates by talking with people in the profession.

Give a range such as between $6 and $8 an hour.

Ask if new employees have a trial period, how long it lasts, and what happens when it ends. Possibilities include the job becomes full time, salary is increased, or benefits are added.

_____

_____

_____

_____

_____

7. Can you tell me about a problem you had on your previous job and how you handled it? _____

Suggestions

This is checking your ability to act maturely and professionally.

Choose an example that shows you handled a situation well.

_____

_____

_____

_____

_____

8. How can you help us make more money or do better as an organization?

Suggestions

Say that you can help by being a highly dependable employee.

Give your definition of dependability: being on time and at work every day; being early and willing to stay late; and getting your work done well and on time.

_____

_____

_____

_____

_____

_____

9. What would you consider your ideal job? _____

Suggestions

Be realistic.

Make sure your answer reflects stability. Employers are looking for people who will stay for at least two years to be worth their training time and effort.

_____

_____

_____

_____

_____

10. Can you tell me why you consider yourself a responsible person? _____

Suggestions

Refer to Chapter 2 on employer expectations.

Give several examples that show you are a reliable person.

_____

_____

_____

_____

_____

11. What are your interests and things you like to do most? _____

Suggestion

Refer to your *Data Minder* pages 5, 14-15.

_____

_____

_____

_____

_____

(continues)

(continued)

12. Why should I offer you the job? _____

Suggestions

State that you feel that you are well qualified.

State that you have the necessary qualifications, such as the following.

Training: I have two years of intensive vocational training in an automotive repair program with over 1,500 hours of hands-on experience.

Education: I have a vocational certificate and high school diploma.

Experience: Talk about your jobs, how long you held them, and what you learned.

Skills: Mention eight or more skills that you do well, that would be necessary for the job, and that would impress the employer.

50 More Problem Questions

The following questions came from a survey of 92 companies that conduct student interviews. Look for questions you would have trouble answering. Then practice answering them using the three-step process.

1. In what school activities have you participated? Why? Which do you enjoy the most?

2. How do you spend your spare time? What are your hobbies?

3. Why do you think you might like to work for our company?

4. What jobs have you held? How were they obtained, and why did you leave?

5. What courses did you like best? Least? Why?

6. Why did you choose your particular field of work?

7. What percentage of your school expense did you earn? How?

8. What do you know about our company?

9. Do you feel that you have received good general training?

10. What qualifications do you have that make you feel that you will be successful in your field?

11. What are your ideas on salary?

12. If you were starting school all over again, what courses would you take?

13. Can you forget your education and start from scratch?

14. How much money do you hope to earn at age 25? 30? 40?

15. Why did you decide to go to the school you attended?

16. What was your rank in your graduating class in high school? Other schools?

17. Do you think that your extracurricular activities were worth the time you devoted to them? Why?

18. What personal characteristics are necessary for success in your chosen field?

19. Why do you think you would like this particular type of job?

20. Are you looking for a permanent or temporary job?

21. Are you primarily interested in making money or do you feel that service to your fellow human beings is a satisfactory accomplishment?

22. Do you prefer working with others or by yourself?

23. Can you take instructions without feeling upset?

24. Tell me a story!

25. What have you learned from some of the jobs you have held?

26. Can you get recommendations from previous employers?

27. What interests you about our product or service?

28. What was your record in the military service?

29. What do you know about opportunities in the field in which you are trained?

30. How long do you expect to work for us?

31. Have you ever had any difficulty getting along with fellow students and faculty? Fellow workers?

32. Which of your school years was most difficult?

33. Do you like routine work?

(continues)

(continued)

34. Do you like work with the same days and hours, or are you willing to work flexible days and hours?

35. In what area do you need the most improvement?

36. Define cooperation.

37. Will you fight to get ahead?

38. Do you have an analytical mind?

39. Are you willing to go where the company sends you?

40. What job in our company would you choose if you were entirely free to do so?

41. Have you plans for further education?

42. What jobs have you enjoyed the most? The least? Why?

43. What are your own special abilities?

44. What job in our company do you want to work toward?

45. Would you prefer a large or a small company? Why?

46. How do you feel about overtime work?

47. What kind of work interests you?

48. Do you think that employers should consider grades?

49. What obstacles have you overcome?

50. What have you done that shows initiative and willingness to work?

Questions You Might Ask an Employer

Most interviewers will invite you to ask questions about the job or organization. The following are questions you can ask during the interview and questions to ask when offered the job.

During the interview:

- Is there a trial period for new employees? How long?

- Are there opportunities for additional training and schooling?

- What tools and equipment are used in this job?

- Is a uniform required?

- How is an employee promoted?

- Could you give me a tour?

© JIST Works, Inc., Indianapolis, IN

List Other Questions You Can Ask

List other questions you can ask to demonstrate your interest in doing well.

_____

_____

_____

_____

_____

_____

When offered the job:

Employers are interested in what you can do for them, not what you want from them. For this reason, it is often wise to avoid certain questions until the job is offered. Examples include questions related to salary, vacations, and benefits.

✔ Phase 4: Closing the Interview

You can close an interview as effectively as you began it. Most people are not offered the job at the close of the first interview. However, you can take certain steps to make a good impression.

Summarize at the Finish

Take a few minutes to summarize the key points of the interview. If any problems or weaknesses came up, state why they will not keep you from doing a good job. Point out strengths you have for the job and why you believe you can do it well.

Ask for the Job

If you are interested in the job, say so. If you want this job, ask for it. Many employers hire one person over another just because one person really wants it and says so.

The Call-Back Close

With the call-back close, you can end the interview to your advantage. It will take some practice. You may not be comfortable with it at first. But it works. Here's how:

1. **Thank the interviewer by name.** While shaking hands, say "Thank you (Mr. or Ms. or Mrs. Jones) for your time today."

2. **Express interest in the job and organization.** Tell the interviewer that you are interested in the position or organization (or both). For example: "The position we discussed today is just what I have been looking for. I am also very impressed with your organization."

3. **Arrange a reason and a time to call back.** If the interviewer has been helpful, he or she won't mind your following up. It's important that you arrange a day and time to call. Never expect the employer to call you. Say something like this: "I'm sure I'll have more questions. When would be the best time for me to get back to you?"

4. **Say good-bye.** After you've set a time and date to call back, thank the interviewer by name and say good-bye: "Again, thank you, Mr. Pomeroy, for the time you gave me today. I will call you next Tuesday morning between 9 and 10 o'clock."

✔ Phase 5: Following Up

You have left the interview and it's over. Right? Not really. You need to follow up! This can make the difference between getting the job or not. Here are some things you must do.

Your follow-up can make the difference between getting the job or not.

- **Send a thank-you note.** As soon as possible after the interview—no later than 24 hours—send a thank-you note. Enclose a JIST Card too. See the information on thank-you notes at the end of this chapter.

- **Make notes.** Write yourself notes about the interview while it is still fresh in your mind. You will not remember details in a week or so.

- **Follow up as promised.** If you said you would call back next Tuesday at 9 a.m., do it. You will impress the interviewer with how organized you are.

✔ *Phase 6: Making a Final Decision*

The interview process is not over until you accept a job. This can sometimes be an easy decision. At other times, deciding can be difficult. Before you take or turn down a job, consider the following points:

- Responsibilities and duties of the job.

- Hours you will have to work.

- Salary and benefits.

- Location and how you will get there. For example, can you take a bus or will you need a car?

- Working conditions.

- Opportunity for advancement.

Once you accept a job verbally, write an acceptance letter that confirms the starting date and time. Be sure to keep a copy of your letter.

Checklist of Steps to Take the Evening Before Your Interview

___ 1. Select and lay out what you plan to wear. Make sure everything is cleaned, pressed, and appropriate. Avoid flashy clothes, excessive jewelry, and strong perfume or cologne.

___ 2. Gather and review the materials you plan to take with you. Include your career portfolio (discussed in Chapter 12), extra copies of your resume, list of references, letters of recommendation, and your *Data Minder.*

___ 3. Make sure you know how to get there on time. Take written instructions or a map if you are not familiar with the interview's location.

___ 4. Take a small notepad and two pens for jotting important notes from your interview.

___ 5. Take extra money to cover unexpected expenses.

___ 6. Get a good night's rest.

Interview Hints: Summing It All Up

The person who gets a job offer is not necessarily the best qualified, but the one who makes the best impression.

- Be neat and clean from head to foot.

- Be knowledgeable about the company.

- Display a positive attitude.

- Smile and be enthusiastic.

- Listen attentively and make direct eye contact.

- Watch your body language.

- Approach the question of salary by giving a range and by knowing the typical salary for the job.

- Don't talk too much and talk yourself out of a job.

- Arrive a few minutes early.

- Get the interviewer to like you.

- Keep looking even if you get an offer. Stop only after you have formally accepted a job.

Thank-You Notes

Sending a thank-you note is a simple act of appreciation, and most people don't take the time to do it. It is simply good manners to send thank-you notes to employers who interview you and to anyone who helps you during your job search.

Thank-you notes also have practical benefits. People who receive them will remember you. But employers say that they rarely get thank-you notes. Employers describe people who do send them with positive terms, such as thoughtful, well organized, and thorough.

A thank-you note won't get you a job you're not qualified for, but it will impress people. When a job opens up, they will remember you. People in your job search network will also be more interested in helping you. If they know of an opening or meet someone who does, they will think of you.

Here are some tips for preparing thank-you notes:

- **Paper and envelope.** Use good-quality notepaper with matching envelopes. Most stationery stores, card shops, and office-supply stores have these supplies. Avoid cute designs. Notepaper with a simple "Thank You" on the front will do. Off-white and buff colors are good.

- **Typed versus handwritten.** You do not always have to send a formal, typed thank-you letter. Handwritten notes are fine unless your handwriting is illegible or sloppy. A neat, written note can be very effective.

- **Salutation.** Unless you are thanking a friend or relative, don't use first names. Write "Dear Ms. Krenshaw" rather than "Dear Lisa." Include the date.

- **The note.** Keep it short and friendly. This is not the place to write, "The reason you should hire me is...." Remember that the note is a thank you for what the person did. It is not a hard-sell pitch for what you want. As appropriate, be specific about when you will next be in contact. If you plan to meet with the person soon, send a note saying you look forward to meeting again and name the date and time.

- **Your signature.** Use your first and last names. Avoid initials and make your signature legible.

- **When to send it.** Send your note no later than 24 hours after your interview or conversation. Ideally, you should write it immediately after the contact while the details are fresh in your mind. Always send a note after an interview, even if things did not go well.

- **Enclosure.** Depending on the situation, a JIST Card is often the ideal enclosure. It's a soft sell and provides your phone number if the person should wish to reach you. ("Gosh, that job just opened up. Who was that person who called me last week?") Make sure your notecards are large enough to hold your JIST Card.

Thank-You Note Examples

2244 Riverwood Avenue
Philadelphia, PA 17963
April 16, 20XXX

Ms. Helen A. Colcord
Henderson & Associates, Inc.
1801 Washington Blvd., Suite 1201
Philadelphia, PA 17993

Dear Ms. Colcord:

Thank you for sharing your time with me so generously today. I really appreciated seeing your state-of-the-art computer equipment.

Your advice has already proved helpful. I have an appointment to meet with Mr. Robert Hopper on Friday. As you anticipated, he does intend to add more computer operators in the next few months.

In case you think of someone else who might need a person like me, I'm enclosing another JIST Card. I will let you know how the interview with Mr. Hopper goes.

Sincerely,

William Henderson

William Henderson

Sept. 30, 20XX

Dear Mr. Hernandez,

Thank you for the interview today. I'm impressed by the high standards your department maintains — the more I heard and saw, the more interested I became in working for your firm.

As we agreed, I will call you next Monday, Oct. 5. In the meantime, please call if you have additional questions.

Sincerely,
Kay Howell

CHAPTER 12

Creating Your Career Portfolio

Unlike a resume, a portfolio contains a variety of documents and items. A career portfolio includes items such as school transcripts, writing and artwork samples, and anything else you think will be helpful in getting a good job.

A career portfolio is designed to help you make the transition from school to work. You can update the portfolio as needed and continue to use it as you seek other employment and education.

A career portfolio will help you present your skills in a format that is easy to recognize and read. For employers, colleges, and training programs, the career portfolio is a tool that helps them screen and select applicants.

The career portfolio is a tool you can use in any situation that calls for a resume or a description of skills and abilities. It gives you a better chance at getting the opportunity you want.

What Are the Benefits of a Career Portfolio?

A career portfolio benefits you in the following ways:

- Helps you define your skills.
- Gives you a better understanding of what employers look for.
- Improves your ability to market yourself.
- Increases your confidence when interviewing.
- Increases your chances for getting a good job and into college.

What Is in a Career Portfolio?

A career portfolio can include a variety of items. Depending on your situation, here are some items you may want to place in your portfolio:

A good portfolio will improve your chances of getting the job you want.

- Letter from principal or school superintendent
- Resume
- High school transcript
- Essay on your career goals
- Summary of skills
- Credentials, such as diplomas and certificates of recognition
- Optional items, such as writing samples and teacher recommendations

Each item should be on a separate page when you assemble your career portfolio. This chapter explains the items above and gives examples.

Letter from Your Principal or Superintendent

The first page of the career portfolio can be a letter from your school principal or other administrator. This letter should be on school letterhead.

The letter's purpose is to confirm that you attended the school. A general letter is usually made available to all students who are preparing career portfolios through a class. If you are developing a portfolio on your own, ask your principal to write this letter for you. A sample is on the facing page.

Neighborhood High School
4444 Friendly Drive
Anytown, New York 12345

To Whom It May Concern:

The faculty of Neighborhood High School appreciates your consideration of the individual presenting this Career Portfolio. Only graduates of our high school or students in good standing have such a document. We trust that you will find this individual to have mastered the various competencies associated with a strong high school curriculum and to have been involved in various school and community activities.

We believe the information contained in this document is accurate and useful to you. In addition, we invite you to visit our high school and our classrooms and observe our commitment to excellence in education. Thank you for your continued support of our graduates and our school system. We believe you will find this individual's performance to be commensurate with the information contained within this portfolio.

Sincerely,

Principal

Resume

You should include the resume that you developed in Chapter 9. Here is a sample resume from one student's portfolio:

JOHN SNOW
234 Steeple Road
Anytown, North Dakota 12345
(222) 333-4444
johnsnow@connect.com

Objective

To receive a Bachelor's Degree in the biology field.

Experience

Panoli's	Ms. Joy Autumn
500 West Farm Drive	338 Bobcat Drive-Apt. C
Anytown, North Dakota 12345	Anytown, North Dakota 12345
(222) 555-6666	(222) 555-7777
June 20XX-November 20XX	November 20XX-May 20XX
Prepared food, ran cashier register,	Cared for three children and
and cleaned the establishment.	performed household duties.

Volunteer Service

Volunteered at the Animal Welfare League in Littletown. Assisted the veterinarian and performed lab work. Groomed, fed, and bathed the animals.

Education

Neighborhood High School
1222 Main Street
Anytown, North Dakota 12345
(222) 111-2222
Received Diploma – 6/XX

Have had the following College Preparatory Courses:

English (3 years)	Anatomy
History (3 years)	Geometry
Biology	Algebra I and II

Achievements

Grade Point Average 3.7 Junior year
Student of the Month for English

Personal

I am a strong person who loves a challenge, enjoys being
around people, and learns quickly.

Transcript

The school transcript is an official document that shows the courses you have taken in high school. It includes your grades and the credits earned, grade point average, days of absences and tardiness, test scores, and may include community service hours completed. It should bear the school's stamp or seal plus the signature of the school administrator.

Follow your school's policy to obtain your transcript. Most employers and college representatives will ask for your transcript, so it is good to include it in your portfolio. Here is a sample transcript:

JANET M. JONES
789 Main Street
Anytown, AZ 12345
PARENT/GUARDIAN: Sue R. Jones
DATE OF BIRTH: 2-5-XX

STUDENT ID: 222-33-4444
ADMISSION DATE: August 25, 20XX
WITHDRAWAL DATE:
GRADUATION DATE: June 6, 20XX
HOMEROOM: 231
COUNSELOR: M. FRANK

COURSE TITLE	FINAL MARK	CRED EARN	COURSE TITLE	FINAL MARK	CRED EARN
YEAR: XX/XX***************GRADE:		09	YEAR: XX/XX**************GRADE:		10
ENGLISH 9	A+	1.000	ENGLISH 10	A-	1.000
GL. CULT & HIST	A	1.000	AMERICAN HISTORY	B+	1.000
ALGEBRA 1	A+	1.000	GEOMETRY	A-	1.000
BIOLOGY	A	1.000	BIOLOGY 2	A	1.000
FRENCH 1	A	1.000	FRENCH 2	A	1.000
PHYS ED 1st SEM	A+	0.250	PHYS ED 1st SEM	A	0.250
PHYS ED 2nd SEM	A-	0.250	PHYS ED 2nd SEM	A	0.250
BEG TYP & KYBD	A	1.000	INTERMED KYBD	B+	1.000
YEAR: XX/XX**************GRADE:		11	YEAR: XX/XX*************GRADE:		12
ENGLISH 11	A-	1.000	ENGLISH 12	A	1.000
CALCULUS	A	1.000	GOVERNMENT	A	1.000
CHEMISTRY	B+	1.000	TRIGONOMETRY	A-	1.000
FRENCH 3	A	1.000	PHYSICS	B	1.000
ART 1st SEM	A	0.500	FRENCH 4	A-	1.000
ART 2nd SEM	A	0.500			

YEAR	ABSENT	TARDY	MO/YR	ATTM CRED	EARN CRED	GPA
XX/XX	2.0	0	06/XX	6.500	6.500	4.000
XX/XX	3.0	1	06/XX	5.000	5.000	3.750
XX/XX	1.0	0	06/XX	5.000	5.000	3.833
XX/XX	1.0	0	06/XX	5.000	5.000	3.800

AZ PROFICIENCY TEST:	DATE PASSED		
MATHEMATICS	OCT. 25, 20XX	CREDITS ATTEMPTED	23.000
CITIZENSHIP	OCT. 25, 20XX	CREDITS EARNED	23.000
WRITING	OCT. 25, 20XX	POINTS EARNED	98.000
		GRADE POINT AVERAGE	3.846
		CLASS RANK	10th/427

VOLUNTEER COMMUNITY SERVICE
  HOURS COMPLETED: 59.5
DATE ISSUED: JUNE 22, 20XX

PRINCIPAL: Mr. Dudley DoGood
Neighborhood High School
Anytown, AZ

Essay on Career Goals

You should develop a one-page essay that describes your career goals and why you decided on them. It should also explain what you plan to do after high school and a "plan B" if the next step doesn't work out. This essay is based on information about yourself and should include things that you can prove or that can be illustrated by examples.

Your career essay gives employers another chance to know more about you and why you chose your career goals. It is important that your essay is well planned, uses correct grammar, and is in an easy-to-follow format. It also should be done with a word-processing program and printed on quality paper.

Make sure your career essay and other portfolio documents are neat and error free.

You may want to include the following information in your essay:

- SAT or ACT scores
- Results of career assessments of interest and aptitude
- A summary of experiences that directly relate to your career goal. Examples of these experiences include the following.
  - ✔ Club memberships, such as a group for future pharmacists
  - ✔ Actual work experience in a related field
  - ✔ Community service relevant to your career goal
  - ✔ Job shadowing, internships, and mentorships in the career field

The following samples were written by high school students and will give you some ideas on writing your essay.

My Future Plans

With the coming of my senior year of high school, the question of what to do with my life surrounds me. This question is to be taken very seriously and requires a lot of thought. Since I was in junior high, I have been thinking of the possible job opportunities that await me. After examining the careers that suit both my talents and my interests, I have come up with a potential plan for my future.

As an "A" student, I enjoy attending school, helping others, and accepting a challenge. For those reasons, I would like to go into the field of teaching. Mathematics seems to be my strongest subject, as I have achieved a perfect grade since entering high school, and I am currently tutoring two of my peers in this subject area. Other courses of interest to me include science and history or government. I have also done extremely well in these areas of study. During my senior year, I plan to take physics, calculus, a history course, and possibly an economics or psychology class at the college level through a postsecondary study program. I believe I could be very successful in this career due to the reasons stated above in this paragraph and also because of my ability to learn quickly and my desire to help people achieve their goals.

If my teaching plan is for some reason unachievable, then my backup plan is to go into a career dealing with financing. This should be another career I should be able to excel in because of my strong mathematics background. Working with numbers is something I can do very well, so I think that this is a good second major.

In all likelihood, I will have a double major in college so that I will have different career choices. It is too risky for me to specialize in one particular field, and then discover that no jobs are available to me. However, whatever I end up pursuing, I know I will do my best at the job, and I intend to offer a lot to that profession.

Preparing for the Future

Graduation is quickly approaching, and I have many important decisions yet to make. I am currently planning to attend a technical school and pursue my desire of becoming a design engineer.

While in the eighth grade, my industrial arts teacher informed me that I had a talent to obtain a successful career in design engineering. Since then I have continued to work with this talent and realized that I really enjoy this field. I have taken or plan to take the following high school courses for preparation in this area: Industrial Arts I, Industrial Arts II, Algebra I, Algebra II, Geometry, Pre-Calculus with Trigonometry, and Physics. I am also computer literate and familiar with the AutoCAD program.

If my plans to become a design engineer do not work out, I will pursue a position as a computer scientist. I enjoy using computers and believe that it is an appropriate alternate career choice. In addition, if I decide to strive for this position, I will need to attend a four-year college.

With much effort and dedication, I believe I will accomplish these goals. In conclusion, the achievements that I obtain today will help me pursue a successful future.

Activity

Write Your Career Essay

Use the worksheet that follows to write a rough draft of your career essay. Your school may have different requirements for your career essay than what we've explained. Your instructor will suggest what to include if it differs from our examples.

Career Essay Worksheet

_____

_____

_____

_____

_____

_____

_____

_____

_____

_____

_____

_____

_____

_____

_____

_____

_____

_____

Summary of Skills

This section gives you an opportunity to summarize your job-related skills in a brief essay or to simply list them.

Refer to Chapter 3 to review your job-related skills.

If you have taken vocational training courses, your teacher can help you identify the job-related skills you mastered. Some examples of vocational training courses are keyboarding, accounting, woodshop, and drafting. You may be in a school that will provide a detailed listing of the skills learned in these courses.

Another way to summarize your skills is to write an essay that describes the good-worker traits or self-management skills you listed in Chapter 3.

The following are samples of these different summaries.

This is a formal version, which is usually provided by your school.

MAJOR COMPETENCY AREAS
of
JOSEPH P. GOODWRENCH

The competencies listed below are those competencies that **Joseph P. Goodwrench** has demonstrated proficiency in and can perform the complete job with normal supervision in the traditional job setting.

BASIC SKILLS

Practice safety procedures and shopkeeping
Maintain tools and equipment
Analyze metals
Cut metals
Repair fasteners
Repair electrical wiring

NONSTRUCTURAL ANALYSIS AND DAMAGE REPAIR

Prepare damaged surface
Replace and adjust outer body panel
Repair and finish steel metal surface
Apply body filling
Perform gas metal arc welding

STRUCTURAL ANALYSIS AND DAMAGE REPAIR

Repair frame
Repair unibody units according to manufacturer's specifications
Repair modular and fixed glass

PLASTICS AND ADHESIVES

Identify and repair rigid and flexible plastic parts

PAINTING AND REFINISHING

Prepare surface
Perform spray gun operations
Mix, match, and apply paint
Identify and correct finish defects
Perform detailing procedures

MECHANICAL AND ELECTRICAL COMPONENTS

Identify lubricants and fluids
Repair electrical systems
Repair brakes and automatic brake system (ABS)
Repair heating and air-conditioning (AC)
Repair cooling system
Repair drive train
Repair fuel, intake, and exhaust systems
Repair active restraint systems
Repair passive restraint systems
Repair supplemental air bag restraint systems according to manufacturer's specifications

SERVICE MANAGEMENT

Manage and operate body shop
Maintain company security requirements
Manage customer relations
Conduct training
Order parts
Prepare estimates
Prepare documentation

COMMUNICATIONS

Apply communications skills

OCCUPATIONAL SKILLS

Apply mathematical skills
Demonstrate business and work ethics

AUTO BODY—2-YEAR PROGRAM
Neighborhood Career Center

This is an example of a simple listing that you can do yourself.

JOSEPH P. GOODWRENCH

Collision Repair Skills

Remove rust

Repair dents

Apply fillers

Smooth surfaces

Grinding

Sanding

Sand blasting

Welding

Air brushing

Masking and painting

Remove, repair and replace:

Belts, struts, batteries, rocker & quarter panels,

fenders, doors, hood, and trunk lid.

Here are two skills summaries in essay form:

As a member of the soccer team, I've learned how to work well with others. There are many different personalities on the team, and I've learned to come together and use teamwork. Without teamwork, it is hard to come out with a victory. I have to listen to my coaches and teammates and follow directions. Along with listening and understanding, I learned to voice my own opinion. Being a member of this team has helped me in respecting other people's ideas and opinions as well. With these skills, I am hoping to become a captain of the team next year.

I am competent in allocating time and following schedules and budgets. I am involved in my church, my community, clubs, and three sports. I also maintain a part-time job. I have learned from experience to make and to keep schedules, and, when conflict occurs, to prioritize. Also, my various activities have taught me the importance of budgeting my paycheck to cover the costs of upkeeping my car, club dues, sports equipment, and savings for college. My participation in these numerous activities gives me the responsibility of being punctual and of managing my time and expenses. Following schedules, budgeting money, and allocating time are just a few of my competencies.

Credentials

This part of your career portfolio contains all formal documents that you have received both in school and from outside sources. You should keep the original documents in your portfolio and make copies to leave with employers.

Put original documents in your portfolio, and make copies for employers.

Your credentials include the following:

- High school diploma
- Certificates of completion
- Certificates of recognition (honor roll, attendance, extracurricular activities, and so on)
- Awards of distinction
- All other honors received

Optional Items

Here is a list of other items that could be included in your career portfolio:

- **School profile.** Describes the educational environment of your school, such as accreditation, grading system, honors courses, and so on.

- **List of accomplishments.** Describes extracurricular and job activities not directly related to your career goal and not included on your resume.

- **Letters of recommendation.** Written by teachers, coaches, advisors, past employers, and anyone else who thinks highly of you.

- **Examples of your work.** Depending on your situation, you can include samples of your art, photographs of a project, audiotapes, videotapes, computer disks, and other media that can provide examples of your work.

- **Sports vita** if applying for a sports scholarship.

- **Documentation of other abilities,** such as musical or artistic skills.

- **Documentation of community service.**

How to Package Your Portfolio

Your career portfolio is a personal reflection of you. The more effort you put into it, the more impressive the final outcome will be. Your portfolio can be the first impression of the following:

Your portfolio can be as simple or as elaborate as you want it to be.

- Who you are

- What you are

- What you want to become

Your portfolio can be as simple or as elaborate as you want it to be. There are many different ways to make a portfolio; only your creativity, time, and budget limit you. For example, you may want to use a three-ring binder or a two-pocket folder, or your high school may provide you with a leather-bound portfolio with your school emblem on it.

Presenting your portfolio will require you to review the contents and be ready to point out the things that will most impress an employer. Be sure to zero in on your strengths. Finally, be prepared with extra copies of your resume and other materials an employer may wish to keep.

Activity

Plan Your Career Portfolio

List the items to include in your portfolio. Your teacher will guide you if your school has additional or different requirements than those listed in this chapter.

Career Portfolio Worksheet

_____

_____

_____

_____

_____

_____

_____

_____

_____

_____

_____

_____

_____

_____

_____

_____

_____

_____

_____

_____

CHAPTER 13

Organizing Your Job Search

Very few job seekers have had any formal training on career planning or job seeking. The few who do have a big advantage over those who don't. Now it's time to put the information from this workbook into action. This chapter will help organize your schedule to make your job search a success.

The Objective of Your Job Search: To Get an Offer for a Good Job

To get a job offer, you must get interviews. To get interviews, you must organize your job search. Before you learn how to organize your job search, let's discuss some important details.

The average job seeker gets about five interviews a month—fewer than two interviews a week. Yet many job seekers using JIST techniques find it easy to get two interviews a day. To do this, you have to redefine what an interview is. Here is our definition:

> ***An interview is face-to-face contact with anyone who has the authority to hire or supervise a person with your skills. The person may or may not have a job opening at the time of the interview.***

With this definition, it is much easier to get interviews. You can now interview with all sorts of potential employers, not just those who have job openings. Remember that you can get interviews by doing the following:

- Use the yellow pages and make about an hour of phone calls. Use the telephone contact script discussed in Chapter 7.

- Drop in on potential employers and ask for an unscheduled interview. Job seekers get interviews this way—not always, of course, but often enough.

- Reach prospective employers with the help of technology—Web sites, e-mail, and fax. (Of course, there's always the U.S. mail too.)

Getting two interviews a day equals 10 a week and over 40 a month. That's 800 percent more interviews than the average job seeker gets. Who do you think will get a job offer more quickly?

Knowing and doing are two different things. So, your job at this time is to pull together what you have learned and make a plan of action.

Activity

Let's Get Started! Create Your Job Search Calendar

To be an effective job seeker, you need a job search calendar. The average job seeker spends about five hours a week actually looking for work. The average person is also unemployed an average of three or more months. People who follow JIST's advice spend much more time on their job search each week. They also get jobs in less than half the average time—often much less than half. So, your job search calendar should include the following:

- The number of hours per week you plan to look for work.

- The days and hours you will look.

- The job search activities you will do during these times.

This activity has three worksheets. The first worksheet helps you make basic decisions about your weekly schedule. The second worksheet shows you how to create your own schedule for one day of the week. The last worksheet helps you put those two parts together to make a job search calendar for one week.

When completing your calendar, assume that you are out of school, unemployed, and looking for a full-time job. In a real sense, you are scheduling your job as if it were a job itself. This calendar will become the model for your actual job search.

Part One: Basic Decisions

Complete the worksheet that follows. Keep these questions and points in mind:

- **How many hours per week?** Once you are out of school, how many hours per week do you plan to look for a job? We suggest at least 25 hours if you are unemployed and looking for a full-time job. If 25 hours seems too many, select a number you feel sure you can keep. Write the number on the bottom of the worksheet.

- **What days will you look?** Mondays through Fridays are the best days to look for most jobs, but weekends are good for some jobs. Put a check mark in the "Yes" column of the worksheet for each day you plan to spend looking for a job.

- **How many hours each day?** You should decide how many hours to spend on your job search each day. It is usually best to put in at least three or four hours each day you look for work. Write the number of hours on the worksheet.

- **What times will you begin and end on each of these days?** The best times to contact most employers are 8 a.m. to 5 p.m. Write these hours on the worksheet.

Basic Decisions About Your Job Search Schedule

Day of Week	Yes ✔	No	Number of Hours per Day	Time Start/Stop	Actual Number of Hours per Day
Sunday				to	
Monday				to	
Tuesday				to	
Wednesday				to	
Thursday				to	
Friday				to	
Saturday				to	

Total Hours per Week _____

Part Two: Your Daily Job Search Plan

You now need to decide how to spend your time each day. This is very important, since most job seekers find it hard to stay productive. You already know which job search methods are most effective, and you should plan to spend more of your time using these. The sample daily schedule that follows has been very effective for those who have used it. It will give you ideas for your own schedule.

Sample Daily Job Search Schedule

7:00 to 8:00 a.m.	Get up, shower, dress, eat breakfast, get ready to go to work.
8:00 to 8:15 a.m.	Organize my workspace. Review schedule for interviews and promised follow-ups. Update schedule as needed.
8:15 to 9:00 a.m.	Review old leads for follow-up. Develop 20 new leads (want ads, yellow pages, networking lists, Internet exploration, and so on).
9:00 to 10:00 a.m.	Make phone calls. Set up interviews.
10:00 to 10:15 a.m.	Take a break.
10:15 to 11:00 a.m.	Make more calls.
11:00 a.m. to noon	Make follow-up calls as needed.
Noon to 1:00 p.m.	Lunch break.
1:00 to 3:00 p.m.	Go on interviews. Make cold contacts in the field. Research potential employers at the library, on the Internet, and at the local bureau of employment services.

Now use the worksheet on the facing page to create your own schedule for a typical day. Use blank sheets of paper as needed.

Job Search Plan for a Typical Day

Time		Plan of Action
Start	End	

Time		Plan of Action
Start	End	

Time		Plan of Action
Start	End	

Time		Plan of Action
Start	End	

Time		Plan of Action
Start	End	

Time		Plan of Action
Start	End	

Part Three: Your Job Search Calendar

Use the information you developed in this chapter to create a calendar for a typical week of looking for work. Look at the following sample and then make your own on the blank worksheet.

Tips for Completing Your Calendar

Your goal is to get interviews. Try to reach that goal in steps. Strive for the following:

■ Three to four interviews during the first week.

■ At least one interview a day during the second week.

■ Two interviews a day during the third and additional weeks. Keep going until success comes your way and you get the job you want.

Weekly Job Search Calendar Worksheet

TIME	DAYS OF THE WEEK						
	Sunday	Monday	Tuesday	Wednesday	Thursday	Friday	Saturday
8:00							
9:00							
10:00							
11:00							
noon							
1:00							
2:00							
3:00							
4:00							
5:00							
6:00							

Weekly Job Search Calendar Worksheet

TIME	Sunday	Monday	Tuesday	Wednesday	Thursday	Friday	Saturday
			DAYS OF THE WEEK				
8:00		Organize day				→	Day off
9:00	Read want ads	Gather old and new leads				→	
10:00		Make phone contacts				→	
11:00	↓	Follow up Get 2 interviews				→	
noon	Lunch	Write/ Send follow-up correspondence			→		
1:00	Explore Internet	Plan afternoon Lunch				→	
2:00			Leave for interview	Drop off resume at printer	Appt. with Lisa at Whitman Co.	Afternoon off!	
3:00		Work on resume	Interview at Fischer Brothers	→	Pick up resume		
4:00	↓	↓	Make final revisions on resume	→	Drop by state employment office	↓	
5:00	Dinner				→		↓
6:00	Read job search books				→		

Activity

Get the Job You Want

Keep the following questions and pointers in mind for getting the job you want. The blank spaces after each section are for your thoughts and notes.

Getting the Job You Really Want Worksheet

1. **Know the job you want.**

   - Do not ask for just "any job you have."

   - Why do you want the job?

   - What skills do you have to do it well?

   - What is the salary range for this type of job?

   - What other jobs require similar skills?

   _____

   _____

   _____

2. **Know what the employer is looking for.**

   - Are you a good, hard worker?

   - Can the employer depend on you to be on time, have good attendance, and do the job?

   - Do you appear to really want this job and say so?

   - If you don't have the best experience, can you overcome this?

   - Will you stay with the organization?

   - Will you be sick or injured?

   - Do your good points outweigh your weaknesses?

   _____

   _____

   _____

(continues)

(continued)

3. Know where to look.

- Small businesses hire about two-thirds of all people. Keep small businesses in mind.

- Spend more time with the most effective job search methods: networking and direct contacts with employers.

- Network with friends, relatives, and acquaintances for job leads and for names of other people to contact.

- Use the yellow pages to find and contact large and small employers.

- Explore company information on the Internet.

- Use traditional job lead sources: want ads, state employment service, and others.

_____

_____

_____

4. Know how to look.

- Always apply alone.

- Organize and make a job search schedule.

- Send thank-you notes.

- Stay in touch with employers and anyone who might help you get job leads.

- Use the phone to save time in setting up interviews and in following up.

- Get lots of interviews. Even if no openings exist now, you may be considered for future ones.

- Do well in interviews and follow up. If you want the job, say so.

_____

_____

_____

5. Think.

- Even if you haven't had a job before, you have abilities and skills that some employer needs.

- Communicate your background and skills on the phone, in person, through your portfolio, and on your JIST Card, resume, and applications.

- Be prepared and know how to answer problem questions in interviews.

- Learn from your failures as well as your successes.

- Find out the reasons you were turned down and overcome them in the next interview.

- If you can't get one type of job, look for another.

- Don't be afraid of asking questions. If you don't know something, ask.

_____

_____

_____

6. **Keep trying.**

- You must apply for work to get it.

- There are openings every day for most skills—though the openings may be hard to find!

- Make your job search into a job itself.

- Spend at least 25 hours a week looking for work.

- Set your goal at getting two interviews a day.

- Don't give up. You are a good person, and you will make it.

_____

_____

_____

7. **A few more tips.**

- Think before accepting the first job offer you receive.

- Don't quit looking just because you have a job offer.

- The more offers you get, the better chance you have at a good job rather than just "a job."

_____

_____

_____

Formula for Job Search Success

Here is the simple formula for getting a good job:

Yellow pages + cold contacts + networking = job leads

Job leads = interviews

Interviews = job offers

Job offers = a job!

© JIST Works, Inc., Indianapolis, IN

CHAPTER 14

Surviving on a New Job and Getting Ahead

Getting a good job is important. But you will also have to keep a job. If you do well, you may be able to move up to a better job—or use what you learn to get a better job. During the years you work, you will have many different jobs. Most people change careers at least three times and hold eight to ten jobs in their working lives. Each new job will bring about changes in your life, and each will present chances to learn and problems to overcome. This chapter will help you get off to a successful start.

Success on the Job

As you begin a new job, you may feel a bit unsure because you don't know what to expect. Will you get along with the other people who work there? Are you dressed right? Will you be able to handle the new responsibilities?

The information in this chapter will help you feel more confident and become a successful employee.

Get Off to a Good Start—Meet Employer Expectations

You were hired because the employer felt you had the skills and abilities needed to get the job done. You will now be expected to become a productive employee. This is your chance to prove that you really do meet all three major employer expectations: appearance, dependability, and skills.

1. Appearance

Here are some things to consider when beginning a new job:

- **Self-image.** Show confidence in the way you present yourself.

- **Dress.** Be neat and clean in your appearance and grooming. Dress appropriately for the type of job you are starting.

- **Personality.** Be natural, friendly, and show respect to your coworkers and supervisors. Don't forget to smile.

- **Communications.** Use good verbal skills when you talk to others. Show your interest by asking questions and being positive.

- **Behavior.** Be cooperative with others and work hard at adjusting to the work routine expected of you. Find someone to help you learn the basics of the job.

2. Dependability

One way to prove that you are worthy of your new job is to show that you are dependable. All employers expect you to be dependable. Make the following a part of your daily job habits:

Allow yourself enough travel time to arrive a few minutes early.

- **Be at work on time.** Arrive a few minutes early. Allow yourself enough travel time by considering the traffic situation and the route you will take.

- **Follow the expected work schedule.** Take only the time allowed for breaks and lunch. Be sure to arrive back at your workstation on the scheduled time or a few minutes early.

- **Know what duties you should be performing.** Be sure that you complete what is expected of you. Ask your supervisor to explain any special procedures or rules to you. Ask for and read at home any personnel and procedural materials related to your job.

- **Don't miss work.** A minor illness (like a cold) is not a good reason for missing work, nor are most personal problems (such as childcare). If you miss more than three days a year for these reasons, it may be too much.

- **Call if you will be absent or late.** If you will be more than a few minutes late or absent for any reason, call in at the beginning of the workday. Talk directly to your supervisor and explain the situation. Do not leave a message. Sometimes, you may be able to call the day before if you think there could be a problem.

3. Skills

Your performance on the job will show the employer whether he or she made the right choice in hiring you. How well will you measure up?

- **Show that you have the skills.** Then apply them daily.

- **Strive to improve your skills.** Develop new ways to do a better job.

- **Seek ways to learn new skills.** Learn all you can from any job you have. Do the job as well as you are able. Look for ways to spend your time more efficiently.

Look for ways to be efficient on the job.

- **Accept responsibility.** Take responsibility for your job and your performance.

- **Know company policies.** Read personnel and procedure manuals.

- **Work fast but carefully.** It is important to work at a steady and quick pace. Find a pace that you can keep up all day without making errors.

- **Be willing to take on additional responsibilities.** Try your best to do something extra when you are asked. Volunteer for tasks that allow you to learn something new.

Other Expectations

- **Stay away from problem employees.** Some people tend to be negative about their jobs. Others do things against the rules, waste time, or in other ways are not good workers. These people may be fun to be with. But spending time with them will affect your performance. Your coworkers and supervisors may begin to see you as a problem. Be friendly, but do not socialize with people like this any more than is necessary.

- **Keep personal activities and problems at home.** You are paid to get a job done. Making personal phone calls, paying bills, coming back late from lunch, or talking to other staff about what you did last weekend are not what you are being paid to do. Although some socializing on the job is common, you can easily overdo it.

> *Limit your personal activities and discussions to breaks, lunch times, and hours outside of work.*

- **Manage children and other family members.** Although children or other family members may be the most important part of your life, they are not the concern of an employer. Make sure that childcare arrangements are in place prior to accepting a job. If your children are in school, arrange childcare so that you do not miss work when they are ill. Strongly discourage personal phone calls except in emergencies. When interviewing for a job, tell employers that you will be a dependable worker and that childcare has been arranged. Assure them that you needn't miss work for this reason.

Why People Get Fired: The Employer's Point of View

Everyone wants to be accepted and successful on a new job. Surviving on the job may mean that you have to change the way you act and some of your attitudes.

One way to survive on a job is to make sure that you avoid the things that get people fired. Here are the top 10 reasons employers give for firing people. The top 3 are listed first.

- **Dishonesty.** This is one of the top reasons employers give for firing someone. More employers are now screening new applicants to eliminate people who have been dishonest with previous employers. Employers don't want to pay someone who steals from them or can't be trusted.

- **Worked too slowly.** This is a major reason for job failure. You can see why: Unproductive employees cost more than they earn. A slow worker is expensive compared to another worker who gets the same job done in less time.

- **Would not follow orders; did not get along with supervisor.** In a battle with a supervisor, you will almost always lose.

- **Unreliable; too many days absent or late.** When an employee is absent, it disrupts the work of others. These people may have to neglect their work to make up for the absent worker. Being late sets a bad example for others and often disrupts others' work.

- **Unable to get along with other workers.** Many workers consider this problem one of the top reasons they don't like their jobs. While few employers list it among the very top reasons for firing someone, it is often a factor. You don't have to like all the people you work with, but it is important that you get along with them.

- **Poor dress or grooming.** The way you look is very important. This is particularly true in office jobs and in jobs where you deal with customers. Poor dress and grooming affect how the employer feels about you. This can be one of many things a terminated employee did not do well.

- **Made too many mistakes.** Someone who makes mistakes can be costly to an employer in many ways. Perhaps another employee has to spend time correcting errors. A customer may become unhappy with the company's products or services as a result of sloppy work. That customer doesn't come back and tells others about the bad experience.

- **Had too many accidents; did not follow safety rules.** Employers do not want to keep people who have accidents or who do not follow safety rules. Accidents can be costly to employers and dangerous to other employees.

- **Could not do the work.** Few people get fired because they could not do the work. Employers tend to hire people they think can do the job and then give them time to learn it.

- **Abuse of alcohol or drugs.** Substance abuse is a major problem in some organizations. A person who abuses alcohol or drugs often gets fired for being unreliable or for some other reason. The employer may not even know the cause of the problem.

There are many reasons an employer might fire a person. Almost any reason can be enough if it is a serious problem. More often, however, people are fired for more than one reason. For example, they may be late to work too often and make too many mistakes in their work.

There are many reasons people lose their jobs. If this happens to you, it is important to learn from the experience and to look for a new job that does not present the same problems.

Activity

Get Off to a Good Start on Your Job

It's important to start a new job with a good attitude and thorough preparation.

Good Start Worksheet

List the issues and problems that may get in your way when starting a new job. Also think of tasks you need to do before starting the job, such as arranging for transportation. Then, list a solution to each issue or the steps you need to take to complete the task. Example: *Issue*—I tend to oversleep. *Solution*—Get to bed earlier and use two alarm clocks.

Issue, Problem, or Task	Solution or Steps to Be Taken

Get Ahead and Move Up on the Job

If you want to advance on your job, you have to do more than the minimum. Here are some extra things you can do to help you get ahead.

1. Dress and groom for a promotion.

- If you want to get ahead in an organization, dress and groom as if you work at the level you hope to reach next. This is not always possible, but at the very least, be clean and well groomed.

- Wear clothes that fit well and look good on you. Copy the clothing styles of others who are successful in the organization. Even when your coworkers see you away from work, present the image you want for yourself at work.

2. Be early and stay late.

- Get to work a few minutes early. Use this time to list what you plan to get done that day. At the end of the day, leave a few minutes after quitting time.

- Be willing to stay late to meet an important deadline. If you stay late, let the boss know. Stay late only when you have an important deadline to meet, unless you are asked.

3. Be enthusiastic.

- Go out of your way to find ways to enjoy your job. Tell others what you like about it, particularly those you work with. Emphasize those parts of your job that you like to do and do well. Share this enthusiasm even in conversations with your friends.

- Make a particular effort to tell your supervisor what you like about your job. This will help you focus on the parts of your job you are most likely to want to do more of. It will also help others notice that you do them well.

4. Ask for more responsibility.

- As soon as you begin a new job, look for ways to learn new things.

- Volunteer to help out in ways you feel will make you more valuable to the organization.

- Let the boss know you want to move up.

- Ask for advice about what you can do to be more valuable to the organization.

5. Ask how you can earn more money.

- In your first week on the job, ask your supervisor to see you for about 30 minutes of private time. When you have his or her attention, say that you want to be more valuable to the organization. Ask what you can do to get a raise as soon as possible. One suggestion is to request special assignments to help develop your skills.

- Before you leave the meeting, ask for a specific future date to go over your progress and what you have to do to get the raise. Ask the boss to give you feedback on your progress from time to time.

6. Ask for training.

- Get as much training as possible! If the training sounds interesting or useful but is outside of your job responsibilities, request it anyway.

Get as much training as possible!

- Define the type of training you need to do your job better, and look for it outside the organization. Explain to your supervisor how the training will help the organization. Ask for help in finding the best training source.

7. Take on difficult projects.

- You won't get much attention unless you do more than what is expected of you. Look for projects that you think you can do well and that would benefit the organization in some clear way.

- Don't promise too much and keep a low profile while you do the work. If no one expects too much, it is easier to be seen as successful even if your results are not as good as you had hoped.

8. Get measurable results.

- Keep records of what you do. Compare them to past performance or the average performance of others in similar situations. If your results look good, send a report to your supervisor. For example, if the number of orders went up 40 percent over the same month last year with no increase in staff, that's a big accomplishment.

- Look for ways to present what you do in numbers, such as dollars saved, percentage of sales increased, number of persons served, number of units processed, and size of budget.

When You Leave a Job

Many people leave their jobs because they don't like the people they work with. People may also be unsatisfied with their jobs for reasons related to money, stress, advancement, and other factors. If you are thinking about leaving your job, here are some points to consider first:

- **Don't just quit.** If the job is not working out for you, ask for a job change within the organization before you give up. If you are unhappy about your job and decide to leave, *do not* talk about it to anyone who works with you until you have found another job. Some people lose their jobs when the boss finds out they are unhappy or planning to leave.

- **Look for another job before quitting.** If possible, begin your job search while you are still employed. You can update your resume, set up interviews before and after work, or take vacation time to look.

- **Notify your employer.** Once you decide to leave, give 30 days notice if at all possible. Two weeks notice is the minimum you should give.

- **Give a positive but honest reason for leaving.** Examples are that you've found a job with more growth opportunity or that you've decided to go back to school. A positive but honest reason is better than complaints, a burst of anger, or not giving any reason at all. You never know when you'll encounter your boss again.

- **Give a written notice.** Give a formal letter of resignation to your supervisor when you tell him or her, in person, that you are leaving. Stress the positive experiences you had and the good feelings you have about the people you worked with. See the sample resignation letter on the next page.

- **Complete all your job responsibilities.** This is especially important if you are working on an individual project or a team effort. Be prepared to train a new person in your job.

- **Leave your present position with a positive attitude.** Say good-bye to people that you have worked with most closely. Don't hold grudges or bad-mouth anyone.

- **Ask for a letter of reference.** Make this request to your supervisor before you leave. If you did well, the letter will be positive, and it is much easier to get it now. If there were problems, at least you will know what he or she will say about you to future employers.

When quitting, leave your job with a positive attitude.

Sample Resignation Letter

Here is a sample letter you can use as a guide. Be sure to include the following:

- Your final date of employment
- Your reason for leaving
- Your personal thanks for the skills you have learned, for the supervisor's support, and for your coworkers' help

47 Mill Run Drive
Orange, California 99999
February 20, 20XX

Ms. Roberta Gordon
Johnson Corporation
2222 Industrial Road
Los Angeles, California 99999

Dear Ms. Gordon:

Please accept this letter as notice of my resignation, effective March 15, 20XX. — **Last date of work**

Reason for quitting — I have accepted a position as quality control assistant with the Harper Corporation and am to report to work on March 30, 20XX.

Thank you for your interest in me, and I want you to know that I will miss — **A personal thank-you** everyone I have worked with here.

Sincerely,

June Hernandez

June Hernandez

The End—and a Beginning

You now know much more about looking for work than most people your age. While this book ends here, so much more is to come for you. We offer a few closing thoughts:

Believe in what you do as special, lasting, and valuable.

- **Don't be afraid to try things.** You will probably have many jobs during the years ahead—some good, some not so good. Each one will teach you something and help you in some way for the future.

- **Decide to do something worthwhile.** Whether it is raising a family or saving old-growth forests, believe in what you do as special, as lasting, as valuable.

- **Work well.** All work is worth doing, so put your energy into it and do it as well as you are able.

- **Enjoy life.** It's sort of the same as having fun, but it lasts longer and means more.

- **Send thank-you notes.** Many people will help you throughout your life in large and small ways. Let them know you appreciate it. The more you give, the more you seem to get in return.

We wish you good fortune in your job search and your life!

APPENDIX

Getting Career Information and Figuring Out a Job Objective

This book assumes that you already have a good idea of the kind of job you want. If you do, this appendix can give you additional information on learning about the many types of jobs in your career area.

If you are not sure what you want to do after high school, that is okay, too. Most young people will try a variety of jobs before they settle into one job or career area. You may also need to earn some money while going to school or feel that you just want to goof off awhile before getting serious about working.

Whatever your situation, it is to your advantage to know how to find out about the many careers available and to concentrate on the ones that seem most interesting. The U.S. Department of Labor provides job descriptions for over 1,100 jobs. That is far more than you can hope to learn about during this course.

There are many ways to find out more about jobs and the right ones for you. This appendix lists some of the most useful ways to explore careers and use career resources.

Counseling Resources

Career counseling: Your school is often a good source of information and advice. Make sure you know what services are available and use them.

Testing resources: You can take a variety of vocational tests to learn more about your interests and abilities. Following are brief comments on the most popular types.

- **Interest tests** allow you to compare the things that interest you to what is done in various careers. Most of these tests will then suggest careers, career clusters, or additional education. Your school may use paper-and-pencil tests or computerized tests.

- **Ability tests** are quite different. They compare what you know and what you can do to the skills of people who already work in various fields. A carpenter, for example, needs to be good with his or her hands and to be able to use various measuring tools. If you do well on the test in manual dexterity and basic math, the test might suggest that carpentry is one field you could do well in. You might not like working with your hands, but the test doesn't consider this. Ability tests may or may not be used in your school. Like interest tests, they can be in the form of paper and pencil or they may be computerized.

- **Other tests** may be available from your school counselor. All these tests can be helpful in some way. But tests are not magic. They can't give you final answers and are often incomplete. You should trust your own sense of what is right for you and do that. Tests can be wrong, and many people are doing—and enjoying—jobs that the tests said they wouldn't be good at. So trust yourself above all else.

Printed Resources

Career materials at the library: Career-related books and journals are available at most libraries. Check your school and public library for information on careers that interest you. Also ask at the library about journals and magazines read by people who work in these fields. These publications are excellent sources for current, field-specific information.

Occupational Outlook Handbook (OOH): We consider this one of the most helpful sources of career infor-mation. Most school counseling offices and libraries have this book. Published by the U.S. Department of Labor, it lists about 250 of the most popular jobs in the country—two-thirds of all people work in these jobs. The *OOH* is updated every two years, so try to get the most current edition.

The jobs are organized into clusters of related occupations. This makes it easy to find jobs that seem interesting and to consider ones that you may not have thought about before. The description for each job includes in-formation on working conditions, fu-ture openings, related jobs, pay scales, training required, and other details. Because it is updated every two years, the information is current, and the descriptions are very well done.

The jobs covered in the *OOH* are listed at the end of this section. Look up the jobs you are interested in and read about them in the *OOH*. Schools can obtain copies of the *OOH* from JIST.

The Guide for Occupational Explora-tion (GOE): Based on a system devel-oped by the Department of Labor, the *GOE* provides a helpful method of ex-ploring careers based on interests, previous experience, skills, and other factors. Newer versions of the *GOE* are published by JIST.

Other Resources

People: Much of what you know about various jobs has probably come from other people. Ask your parents and others what they do and do not like about their jobs. Then compare this to your own likes and dislikes. When you identify a job that really interests you, find someone who does that work and ask him or her to tell you more about it.

The Internet: The Internet offers an enormous amount of information on careers and education. Ask your teacher or a librarian for good sites for this information.

Entry-level and volunteer jobs: Many young people can get jobs in fields that interest them for careers. If you want to work in the medical field, for example, try to get a job in a hospital or other medical facility. Hospitals also use volunteers in various roles, and you may be able to turn unpaid experience into a paying job.

Working your way up: You may have to start at the bottom and work your way up. Young people can often take an entry-level job and use it to show that they can work hard and be trusted.

For example, if you have never managed a business, few employers would hire you to run one. But you might be able to get a job as a stock clerk and then learn as much as possible about the business. Let the employer know that you want more responsibility. Be willing to take on new tasks. Even if you can't move up in that job, you can use what you learn to get a better job in the future.

Occupational Outlook Handbook Occupations Listing

Check jobs in the list that seem interesting to you. Then look up the description for the jobs that interest you most in the *Occupational Outlook Handbook*. The brief descriptions there include useful information on working conditions, skills needed, education and training required, earnings, related jobs, and more.

Executive, Administrative, and Managerial

Accountants and auditors
Administrative services and facility
  managers
Advertising, marketing, and public
  relations managers
Budget analysts
Construction and building
  inspectors
Construction managers
Cost estimators
Education administrators

Employment interviewers, private
  or public employment service
Engineering, natural science, and
  computer and information sys-
  tems managers
Farmers and farm managers
Financial managers
Funeral directors and morticians
General managers and top
  executives
Government chief executives and
  legislators
Health services managers
Hotel managers and assistants
Human resources, training, and
  labor relations specialists and
  managers
Industrial production managers
Inspectors and compliance officers,
  except construction
Insurance underwriters
Loan officers and counselors
Management analysts
Property, real estate, and
  community association managers
Purchasing managers, buyers, and
  purchasing agents
Restaurant and food service
  managers

Professional and Technical

Air transportation-related
Aircraft pilots and flight engineers
Air traffic controllers

Engineers and engineering technicians
Engineers
  Aerospace engineers
  Chemical engineers
  Civil engineers
  Electrical and electronics engineers
  Industrial engineers, except safety
    engineers
  Materials engineers
  Mechanical engineers
  Mining engineers, including mine
    safety engineers
  Nuclear engineers
  Petroleum engineers
Engineering technicians

Architects, surveyors, and drafters
  Architects, except landscape and
    naval

  Drafters
  Landscape architects
  Surveyors, cartographers, photo-
    grammetrists, and surveying
    technicians

Computer, mathematical, and operations research
  Actuaries
  Computer systems analysts,
    engineers, and scientists
  Computer programmers
  Mathematicians
  Operations research analysts
  Statisticians

Scientists and science technicians
Life scientists
  Agricultural and food scientists
  Biological and medical scientists
  Conservation scientists and
    foresters

Physical scientists
  Atmospheric scientists
  Chemists
  Geologists, geophysicists, and
    oceanographers
  Physicists and astronomers
Science technicians

Legal
  Lawyers and judicial workers
  Paralegals and legal assistants

Social scientists
  Economists and marketing research
    analysts
  Psychologists
  Urban and regional planners
  Social scientists, other

Social and recreation workers
  Human service workers and
    assistants
  Recreation workers
  Social workers

Clergy
  Protestant ministers
  Rabbis
  Roman Catholic priests

Teachers and instructors, counselors, and library occupations
  Adult and vocational education
    teachers

Archivists, curators, museum technicians, and conservators
College and university faculty
Counselors
Instructors and coaches, sports and physical training
Librarians
Library technicians
School teachers—kindergarten, elementary, and secondary
Special education teachers

Health diagnosticians
Chiropractors
Dentists
Optometrists
Physicians
Podiatrists
Veterinarians

Health assessment and treating
Dietitians and nutritionists
Occupational therapists
Pharmacists
Physical therapists
Physician assistants
Recreational therapists
Registered nurses
Respiratory therapists
Speech-language pathologists and audiologists

Health technologists and technicians
Cardiovascular technologists and technicians
Clinical laboratory technologists and technicians
Dental hygienists
Electroneurodiagnostic technologists
Emergency medical technicians and paramedics
Health information technicians
Licensed practical nurses
Nuclear medicine technologists
Opticians, dispensing
Pharmacy technicians and assistants
Radiologic technologists
Surgical technologists

Communications-related
Announcers
Broadcast and sound technicians
News analysts, reporters, and correspondents

Public relations specialists
Writers and editors, including technical writers

Visual arts and design
Designers
Photographers and camera operators
Visual artists

Performing arts
Actors, directors, and producers
Dancers and choreographers
Musicians, singers, and related workers

Marketing and Sales
Cashiers
Counter and rental clerks
Demonstrators, product promoters, and models
Insurance sales agents
Manufacturers' and wholesale sales representatives
Real estate agents and brokers
Retail salespersons
Retail sales worker supervisors and managers
Securities, commodities, and financial services sales representatives
Services sales representatives
Travel agents

Administrative Support, Including Clerical
Adjusters, investigators, and collectors
Bank tellers
Communications equipment operators
Computer operators
Court reporters, medical transcriptionists, and stenographers
Information clerks
  Hotel, motel, and resort desk clerks
  Interviewing and new accounts clerks
  Receptionists
  Reservation and transportation ticket agents and travel clerks
Loan clerks and credit authorizers, checkers, and clerks
Mail clerks and messengers

Material recording, scheduling, dispatching, and distributing occupations
Dispatchers
Shipping, receiving, and traffic clerks
Stock clerks
Office and administrative support supervisors and managers
Office clerks, general
Postal clerks and mail carriers
Records processing occupations
  Billing clerks and billing machine operators
  Bookkeeping, accounting, and auditing clerks
  Brokerage clerks and statement clerks
  File clerks
  Human resources clerks, except payroll and timekeeping
  Library assistants and bookmobile drivers
  Order clerks
  Payroll and timekeeping clerks
Secretaries
Teacher assistants
Word processors, typists, and data entry keyers

Service

Cleaning, buildings, and grounds service
Janitors and cleaners and institutional cleaning supervisors
Landscaping, groundskeeping, nursery, greenhouse, and lawn service occupations
Pest controllers

Food preparation and beverage service
Chefs, cooks, and other kitchen workers
Food and beverage service occupations

Health service
Dental assistants
Medical assistants
Nursing and psychiatric aides
Occupational therapy assistants and aides
Physical therapist assistants and aides

Personal service

Barbers, cosmetologists, and related workers

Flight attendants

Home health and personal care aides

Preschool teachers and child-care workers

Private household workers

Veterinary assistants and nonfarm animal caretakers

Protective service

Correctional officers

Fire fighting occupations

Guards

Police and detectives

Private detectives and investigators

Mechanics, Installers, and Repairers

Electrical and electronic equipment mechanics, installers, and repairers

Computer, automated teller, and office machine repairers

Electronic home entertainment equipment repairers

Electronics repairers, commercial and industrial equipment

Telecommunications equipment mechanics, installers, and repairers

Other mechanics, installers, and repairers

Aircraft mechanics and service technicians

Automotive body repairers

Automotive mechanics and service technicians

Coin, vending, and amusement machine servicers and repairers

Diesel mechanics and service technicians

Farm equipment mechanics

Heating, air-conditioning, and refrigeration mechanics and installers

Home appliance and power tool repairers

Industrial machinery repairers

Line installers and repairers

Maintenance mechanics, general utility

Millwrights

Mobile heavy equipment mechanics

Motorcycle, boat, and small-engine mechanics

Musical instrument repairers and tuners

Construction Trades

Boilermakers

Bricklayers and stonemasons

Carpenters

Carpet, floor, and tile installers and finishers

Cement masons, concrete finishers, and terrazzo workers

Construction equipment operators

Drywall installers and finishers

Electricians

Elevator installers and repairers

Glaziers

Hazardous materials removal workers

Insulation workers

Painters and paperhangers

Plasterers and stucco masons

Plumbers, pipefitters, and steamfitters

Roofers

Sheet metal workers and duct installers

Structural and reinforcing metal workers

Production

Assemblers

Precision assemblers

Blue-collar worker supervisors

Fishers and fishing vessel operators

Food processing

Butchers and meat, poultry, and fish cutters

Forestry, conservation, and logging

Inspectors, testers, and graders

Metalworking and plastics-working

Jewelers and precious stone and metal workers

Machinists and numerical control machine tool programmers

Metalworking and plastics-working machine operators

Tool and die makers

Welders, cutters, and welding machine operators

Plant and systems operators

Electric power generating plant operators and power distributors and dispatchers

Stationary engineers

Water and wastewater treatment plant operators

Printing

Bindery workers

Prepress workers

Printing press operators

Textile, apparel, and furnishings

Apparel workers

Shoe and leather workers and repairers

Textile machinery operators

Upholsterers

Woodworking

Miscellaneous production

Dental laboratory technicians

Electronic semiconductor processors

Ophthalmic laboratory technicians

Painting and coating machine operators

Photographic process workers

Transportation and Material Moving

Busdrivers

Material moving equipment operators

Rail transportation occupations

Taxi drivers and chauffeurs

Truckdrivers

Water transportation occupations

Handlers, Equipment Cleaners, Helpers, and Laborers

Job Opportunities in the Armed Forces

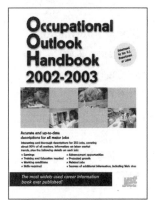

JIST Order and Catalog Request Form

Purchase Order #: _____ (Required by some organizations)

Billing Information

Organization Name: _____

Accounting Contact: _____

Street Address: _____

_____

_____

City, State, Zip: _____

Phone Number: (   ) _____

Shipping Information with Street Address (If Different from Above)

Organization Name: _____

Contact: _____

Street Address: (We *cannot* ship to P.O. boxes) _____

_____

_____

City, State, Zip: _____

Phone Number: (   ) _____

Please copy this form if you need more lines for your order.

Phone: 1-800-648-JIST
Fax: 1-800-JIST-FAX
World Wide Web Address:
http://www.jist.com

Credit Card Purchases: VISA_____   MC_____   AMEX_____

Card Number: _____

Exp. Date: _____

Name As on Card: _____

Signature: _____

Quantity	Order Code	Product Title	Unit Price	Total
	—	**Free JIST Catalog**	**Free**	—

jist *Publishing*

_____

8902 Otis Avenue
Indianapolis, IN 46216

Shipping / Handling / Insurance Fees

In the continental U.S. add 7% of subtotal:
- Minimum amount charged = $4.00
- Maximum amount charged = $100.00
- FREE shipping and handling on any prepaid orders over $40.00

Above pricing is for regular ground shipment only. For rush or special delivery, call JIST Customer Service at 1-800-648-JIST for the correct shipping fee.

Outside the continental U.S. call JIST Customer Service at 1-800-648-JIST for an estimate of these fees.

Payment in U.S. funds only!

Subtotal	
+5% Sales Tax *Indiana Residents*	
+Shipping / Handling / Ins. (See left)	
TOTAL	

JIST thanks you for your order